Christine Reed

FIBER ARTS

FIBER ARTS

Macrame, crochet, wrapping, coiling, weaving

DIANE PHILIPPOFF MAURER

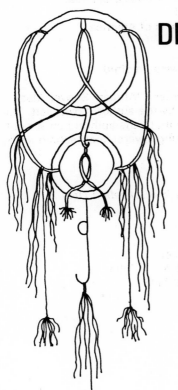

CHILTON BOOK COMPANY Radnor, Pennsylvania

Fiberworks on the cover: Center: "African Shovel Mask—Morani," macrame relief work by the author. Lower left: "Lichen Bed," sculptural coiled work by the author. Lower right: "Rainbow U.S.A.," sculpture using several fiber techniques by Ruth Geneslaw.

Library of Congress Cataloging in Publication Data

Maurer, Diane Philippoff.
  Fiber arts.

  (Chilton's creative crafts series)
  1. Textile crafts. 2. Fiberwork. I. Title.
TT699.M393 1978   746   78-7143
ISBN 0-8019-6659-0
ISBN 0-8019-6660-4 pbk.

1 2 3 4 5 6 7 8 9 0   7 6 5 4 3 2 1 0 9 8

To my parents
who loved black sheep before I did.

CONTENTS

ACKNOWLEDGMENTS

I'd like to thank:

Those fiber artists who permitted me to include their inspiring works in this book, especially Ruth Gowell and Anne Mitchell who gave freely of their expertise, as well.

Sally Kirkendale for her midnight typing of the manuscript, Judith Wrend for her assistance with crochet projects and architectural drawings, Paul Maurer and Christopher Leaman for developing and printing my photographs, and Virginia Moore English for illustrating the work.

Thanks, too, to my student and friend, Hazel Humphreys Richmond, whose enthusiasm suggested this book and to my daughter Jenny, who brought me flowers and helped me to see.

FIBER ARTS

CREATING WITH FIBER

Weavers bear children on my front porch each year, suspending leathery egg sacs in their ever-spreading webs. A few years ago, I would probably have hurried past the spider's pottery and fiberwork and totally missed an opportunity to see beyond the clutter of my daily life. I would not have allowed the spider's creative energy to touch me, to fill me with wonder, to nourish my own creative spirit. But that was before I heard the discordant sounds of my life which led me to rearrange priorities. Today I pause as I pass by and smile to the spiderlings who wait for flies and weave my inspirations.

In our rush to accomplish and produce, we can easily lose contact with the simple pleasures and abilities we once knew. As we grow older and more intellectual, we often neglect an important part of ourselves—our creative spirit. Given a ball of string and a few instructions, a child will engage in play and create something, delighted with the experience and the result, until the adults inevitably ask, "What is it?" We seem to need an inordinate amount of labels. Given a ball of string and the same instruction, most adults will self-consciously agonize over what to create unless given a concrete plan with which to fashion something useful. Adult life is full of restraints and priorities and a lot of "shoulds" that not only block our abilities to play, but our abilities to see with our hearts and to create with our hands.

Often I hear people say, "I wish I were creative. . . ." There's no need to lament the fact that you're not creative, because we are all naturally creative. Instead, lament the fact that for years you were deluded into believing that spider webs should be swept away as dirt, or that adults who gazed in wonder over the intricate scale patterns of a dead fish were a little crazy, or that only a chosen few were capable of artistic expression. Lament the fact that you were led to believe that rocks should be removed from your lawn and used as land fill or used as paperweights, or used to create a border for your garden, when, in fact, their greatest use may involve touching them only with your eyes and letting their meandering veins, sharp points, and quiet rounds stimulate your imagination.

Much creativity is buried beneath the intellectual and technical debris our lives produce, but we can reestablish a harmonious place in the natural world by seeing more with our hearts, listening more to our emotions, and trusting more in our intuitions. If we quiet ourselves enough to savor impressions and images instead of being so preoccupied with facts and details, the creative spirit in each of us will flower again.

This book is about fiber art and about involving you, the artist, body and spirit in the creation of a work. Through it you can learn to spin your own wool yarns, forage field and wood to find dye plants producing subtle moods of color, and prepare potent dye baths to color your handspun fibers. You will learn to transform commercial or handspun yarns into fiberworks as you practice technique and design, exploring macrame, wrapping, coiling, crochet, and weaving as two-dimensional, relief, and sculptural media. This book will help you read the design principles evident in nature and show you how to resurrect rusted tools and fallen branches to frame or enhance a fiber statement. Photographic illustration of professional fiber artists' work and a study of the sources for inspiration abounding in the natural and manmade worlds will further aid you in forming your own designs and expressing your individuality through fiber art.

FIBER AS AN EMERGING ART FORM

Fiberwork has been an accepted art form for thousands of years. Anyone can see that the medieval tapestries which hang in museums are much more than folk expressions or handicraft. Nevertheless, the idea of fiber as a serious art form was not readily accepted by the contemporary art world. Over a decade ago, fiber artists began taking to art galleries new forms of art constructed with ancient techniques. But the fine arts community, used to seeing fiberwork in terms of crocheted afghans, macrame belts, and woven pillows, considered the new artists as interlopers. Fiber was not held to be

a fine arts medium—it was clearly a crafts medium. Artists were seers, while craftspeople were workers who provided beautiful utilitarian objects for their people or created inexpensive gifts to sell at bazaars. Why on earth craftspeople were trying to force their work upon the art scene was anybody's guess. Art show prospecti soon carried bold headlines—NO CRAFTS.

Having seen my share of door-stop dollies and macrame plant hangers, and being seriously involved in fiberwork on a different level, I decided to enter one of the shows anyway and find out just what "NO CRAFTS" meant. I went to a prominent art center some seven years ago, found the exhibitions director and explained that I had brought a piece of fiberwork to be juried for the show. "No crafts will be shown," she snapped. I went into my medieval tapestry routine. "Did you bring a medieval tapestry?" she inquired. Her partner, holding a watercolor snow scene, snickered. "No," I replied, "but I do have an eight-foot primordial bog in a pick-up truck and need help getting it in here."

That was the end of the encounter, since the exhibitions people refused to deal with me any further. I returned home with my unseen work and a story to share. A painter friend responded by creating a self-portrait on wood, cutting it to pieces with a jigsaw and entering the puzzle in the next competition along with a political statement about art. A sculptor friend bent metal rods to create a 200-pound weaving and asked the question, "If it's woven in steel instead of wool, is it art?" Test cases arose frequently in those days as known serious artists left their brushes and canvases to try fiber and find out what all the noise was about. We had allies and enemies and lots of laughter and tears before judges and gallery owners, aroused by the controversy, stepped forward to make public statements about their policies concerning craft and art. The differentiation between handicrafts on the one hand and fine crafts or art became a point for consideration as work was finally judged on its own merits instead of on the previous reputation of the medium from which it was created. The separation between the serious artist and the serious craftsperson narrowed as fiber artists, encouraged by the publicity and the air of change, produced monumental fine works and participated in widely exhibited shows such as Objects U.S.A. and Convergence, contributing fiber pieces of such high quality that they were applauded in art reviews across the nation.

But change was slow to reach some areas, and as recently as three years ago the judges in a Philadelphia show awarded one of my masks (fig. 1-2) an honorable mention in a sculpture competition and then sought me out to explain their dilemma. The mask was a fine work, they said, but they had difficulty deciding whether it actually qualified as relief sculpture. As it was not meant to be worn, it was probably not craft, but as it was created of fiber, it might not be sculpture either. I received their congratulations, apologies, and the name and address of a colleague of theirs who shared an affliction similar to mine—he was a potter who created nonfunctional pots!

Today such confusions are rare. Fiber vies successfully with stone and steel as an acceptable sculpture medium, and nonfunctional pieces are seen as art and not as oddities. We must thank

Fig. 1-2 "Sulimani," the contro-
versial nonfunctional mask.

those judges and gallery owners who were willing
to risk their reputations by showing new fiber
pieces and those artists who continued to create
them, despite the prejudice against them, for the
fact that today fiber artists are no longer seen as
second class artists but seers in their own rights
whose work is judged not on its usefulness but as
an aesthetic product of the imagination.

MATERIALS

WORKING WITH NATURAL FIBER

Creating, especially with natural fiber, is a freeing experience. One works closely with a material, seeing its color, feeling its coarseness or silkiness, and often, as with goat hair, smelling it as well. All the sensations are stimulating to the imagination, a fact which has lured many a painter or potter to a new medium. The pliable nature of yarn lends itself to two-dimensional, relief, or sculptural forms.

Natural yarns are derived from animals or from plants. Animal yarns, some of which are pictured in fig. 2-1, include wool, cow, goat, and horse hair, and silk from worms. Human hair yarn is also available and spun dog hair can be used as well (but beware the canine "jurors" at outdoor shows!). Various wools, for weaving and crochet, are readily available in any yarn store. The more exotic animal hair fibers, useful as weft materials for weaving and coiling, are usually imported from the Scandinavian countries or from Greece. Both soft and coarse animal fibers, spun alone or mixed with wool, can be purchased at a weaver's supply store.

Plant yarns (fig. 2-2) are numerous, including sisal, jute hemp, flax, cotton, linen, and manila. The plant yarns, especially coarse jute, sisal, and manila, which are often used for macrame, are generally less expensive and more readily available than animal fibers. Most can be found on the shelves in any hardware store. Fine linens and cottons, which make excellent warp cords for weaving, can be found in most craft stores.

Each yarn has particular qualities which influence its use in a fiberwork. Some yarns, such as jute and cotton, will withstand much stress and twisting; others, such as goat hair, will break apart if handled too severely. It's discouraging to find cords breaking halfway through a knotted hanging or the sharp edge of a piece of sculpture curling after a few weeks. It's best, therefore, to consider and to learn the nature of each yarn before begin-

Fig. 2-1   Animal fiber yarns.   Fig. 2-2   Plant fiber yarns.

ning a work. Yarn should be judged for ply, elasticity, strength and durability, and rigidity by handling a small length of it.

Ply

Ply is the number of fiber strands that are twisted together to make the yarn. I find untwisting a piece of yarn is a good way to judge its usefulness. Some three-ply jute is tightly twisted and difficult to undo; others will readily unply and will show uneven spinning, thick at one point and terribly thin and weak at another. The latter cord would probably be fine used as a weft for weaving, but would not cooperate at all in a macrame piece. In general, a single-ply yarn is weaker than a yarn with two or more plies. But the strength of a multi-ply yarn depends not so much on the number of plies as on the quality of the fiber and how tightly the plies are twisted.

Elasticity

Most everyone is aware of the elastic properties of wool yarn, but few people realize that jute and cotton will stretch as well. Measuring a length of cord held taut and the *pulled* taut can give surprising results. Elasticity is especially important to take into account if you intend to work with specific dimensions in mind. A metal rod at the bottom of a long wall hanging will give sharp definition to floating or loose cords, but in an elastic material it may also create a work several inches longer than expected.

Durability

Just as no one wants a hanging which also carpets the floor, no one is especially eager to own a plant hanger which self-destructs in two months. You can test a cord and deem it suitable for a tug of war and still be fooled. Some plant fibers are especially susceptible to decomposition from the environment. Using tarred hemp will prolong the life of an outdoor hanging, but even indoor conditions can damage yarn. After spending years creating primarily with jute yarn because of its rough texture and its low cost, I was shocked to learn that several museums would no longer consider buying works done in this material. Even in a museum's controlled environment, jute was found to decompose after several decades. Ancient linen tapestries, however, can be seen in museums throughout the world. Work in linen if you can afford it and consider, when placing a piece, that dust, smoke, moisture, and moths should be avoided if possible.

Rigidity

Rigidity refers to how well a fiber cord will hold its shape. Testing for rigidity is sometimes difficult. Any cord which you have to wear gloves to handle is obviously coarse enough to hold a shape. Other yarns may seem quite stiff at first but will become limp after a few weeks. Cotton seine and jute are prime offenders. One can create a well-defined wrapped curve in either material, but wire reinforcement is often necessary to maintain it. Handling alone softens both materials, and you will notice that the cords at the start of a knotted work are more stiff than the soft nappy cords at its finish. Wire or a spray starch is sometimes necessary to support appendages even on two-dimensional work. Wool wrapped over a core of heavy sisal will maintain a basket shape, but wool wrapped over a core of wool will often lose definite form. Experimenting with rigidity, however, is often fruitful—a simple woven basket can relax into a wonderful free-form sculpture.

WORKING WITH NATURE'S GIFTS

A walk through the woods or along a beach can be especially meaningful to a fiber artist. In addition to providing loads of ideas for nature-inspired fiberworks and plenty of plants for dye stuffs, our natural environment is rife with materials to incorporate into any work (see fig. 2-3). (All found materials should be used sparingly, of course, if they're meant to complement rather than to become the main focus of a piece.)

Driftwood and fallen branches abound with knot holes, worm tracks, and burl formations. Smoothed by the sand or rough with clinging bark, they are easily employed as a base for, or a fine addition to, hangings. A quick test for strength and a once over for any inhabitants is all that's necessary before use.

Seeds, nuts, and pods are found everywhere in varying sizes and shapes. Often the seeds inside a large pod will still be of drilling size and even more beautiful than the pod which holds them. Accidentally stepping on an ear pod from Florida revealed several large seeds with circular stripes in shades of brown. Except for the poisonous castor bean seed, they're the most beautiful I've found. An electric drill with a bit the size of the yarn you wish to accommodate does the hole-boring job nicely if the nut or seed is clamped securely in a small vise. A vise clamped too tightly will, of course, act as a nutcracker. You can use either discretion with the vise, or else the seeds which fall from the cracked pod.

Vines and grasses can be wrapped into a fiberwork or used as actual weaving materials. If you cut grasses instead of digging them up, you can return to the same spot later for another crop. Remember that grasses are not known for their longevity and should not be used in a work through which you hope to achieve immortality. Grasses should, of course, be thoroughly dried before use, as they will mold if used fresh. Beware, too, of expansion. A weaver friend in New Orleans swears that she wove a vest out of Spanish moss and returned from a vacation to find that it had grown into a huge coat and had taken over her entire closet.

Shells and fish bones often contain natural holes, but they, too, can be drilled with ease if necessary. Fish vertebrae have especially beautiful shapes, and if soaked for several hours in a weak solution of bleach and water and then sun-dried, they will be quite pleasant to work with.

If employed properly, feathers can give a primitive feeling to a work without overpowering the fiber itself. They are readily available today in craft stores around the country and from feather companies. A few years ago, when feathers were not as much in demand, I found several ways of locating them. For those purists among you and for those who would rather not support the slaughter of birds (feathers, after all, look most beautiful on the bird which grew them), I pass on the following: Animal parks containing aviaries will always yield a few choice feathers. Farmyards, during moulting season, will yield bags full. Most farmers will be cooperative in letting you gather the castoffs from ducks, guinea hens, and chickens, especially if you treat yourself to a purchase of fresh eggs as well. I own three plucky brown and white hens who supply lots of curved and fluffy pin feathers each year, in addition to breakfast each morning. Consider chicken farming, if you have the space.

Depending upon your location and spirit of adventure, another possibility exists. A highway cuts through woods and fields a few miles from my house and for years I'd winced at the dead pheasants I'd seen killed by passing cars. Finally one day I realized that it would be much more fitting to use bird feathers in an artwork and to give the bird a proper burial than to leave it to decay along the roadside. With a plastic bag and a queasy stomach I lifted my first pheasant from the road, checked it for bird mites, brought it home, plucked it, and promptly lost the body to a hungry racoon. The second time was infinitely easier, and those two birds supplied me with feathers for over a year.

It's a good idea to seek permission before removing any natural materials from state or federal forests. I've learned recently that some states also

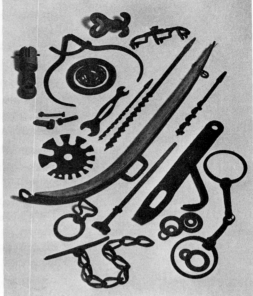

Fig. 2-3 Natural found objects can inspire or become part of a fiberwork.

Fig. 2-4 Manmade objects can also inspire a design or become part of the piece.

require a license to remove a dead bird from the road. My informant was a taxidermist who wanted to charge me the bargain rate of twenty dollars to skin a pheasant. The laws are made to protect birds and taxidermists as well—check your state codes or body-snatch after dark.

WORKING WITH FOUND OBJECTS

Found objects are easily incorporated into a fiberwork and lend another dimension to expression. Branches, bones, and seeds enhance a natural statement, but old tools and farm implements can be equally expressive and can, themselves, serve as inspirations (see fig. 2-4). A primitive animal trap with sharp spikes suggested to me a sculpture entitled "Night Dreams." As I knotted and wrapped over it, the protruding teeth played against sprays of feathers dangling from fiber spines and portrayed nightmares mingling with and interrupting the fantasies of the dream world.

It's exciting to see tools, so often symbols of a destructive technology, functioning constructively in an aesthetic way. It's great fun, too, to welcome each morning as the start of another treasure hunt—for castoff finds are everywhere.

Old nuts, bolts, washers, and lengths of metal tubing are often found in the street, near railroad tracks, in your friend's cellar, and, almost always, in your mechanic's garage. Usually a simple scrubbing and washing with a wire brush will remove loose flakes of rust and ready them for use as a wrapped addition or a unique bead in a fiberwork. I love the beautiful brown/red color and pitted appearance of rusted iron and feel that shellac ruins the special character of the metal. If you intend to use a heavily rusted piece in a pure white work, however, you might consider giving it a coat of shellac to prevent discoloring the yarn.

It's absolutely amazing to see how many shovels are discarded each year due to broken handles. Forked implements, too, are rarely repaired. A trip through most any community on a large trash removal day will yield a few free tools. Shovel blades can become masks, old boot scrapers can be transformed into antlers—the possibilities are endless.

Very inexpensive, mystifying iron objects show up in garage sales and thrift shops every week. Antique shops house some fantastic old scales, pulleys, and hames, often at reasonable prices. Horse and farm auctions sometimes feature boxes of ornate bits at ridiculously low prices, and friends and relatives can come up with some amazing finds when they know you're interested in such junk.

No one will have any trouble finding rusted tools, except perhaps in Amish country. The problem will most likely be that you've found the perfect piece and it's not rusted *enough.* You can speed the oxidizing process by soaking the metal in vinegar for a few days and then exposing it to the elements. Then, too, you could bury it for a while and work on something else.

MACRAME

TOOLS AND WORKING METHODS

Macrame students sometimes find themselves confused about what kind of working surface to use. Foam pads, cork with T-pins, and grid imprinted fiberboard all claim to making macrame a snap, but T-pins pull out of surfaces when stress is applied, and properly executed knots require pulling cords tightly. Unless you're using a graph with a pattern for a work which must be an exact dimension, graphboard should be barred from your studio. If you want something that looks machine-made it's easier to just go out and buy it. You can't put your personality into a piece when you're staring at a grid indicating where you should line up your next knot. Useful at first, these shortcuts soon become crutches which prevent you from learning to handle your medium.

Working While Seated

To work at knotting while seated you'll need the following supplies:

    large board (I use a 15" × 21" bread board)
    12" dowel to knot from (mounting bar)
    2 nails with large heads to keep the dowel in
      place
    scissors
    yarn
    yardstick

These supplies are pictured in fig. 3-1. Optional supplies would be a weaving needle for wrapping or adding cords, rubber bands for making cords shorter, and push pins to temporarily hold work in place if you feel this necessary.

Working While Standing

I recommend working while standing whenever possible, because the further your work is from the ground the less problem you'll have with tangling.

Fig. 3-1 Macrame supplies, showing the mounting bar positioned on the knotting board.

Except for the board, your supplies will be the same as those for seated work. To work while standing outdoors, you can place a dowel between tree branches or on nails as was done on the bread board. Indoors, if you have an old door in your home that you could unwincingly nail into you're in fine shape; otherwise, wall hooks or pegboard and hooks (if you can stand looking at all the little holes) will hold your dowel securely.

Estimating Lengths of Yarn

Determining the length of cord you'll need for a hanging is somewhat tricky. In general it's best to figure that each cord should be eight times the length of the intended work *before* the cord is doubled and strung on your dowel. For a 3-foot hanging, each cord should then be 24 feet long; but after the cords are attached to the dowel you will be working with 12-foot strands. Tightly knotted works use much more yarn than hangings with loose unknotted areas, and thicker cords are used up more quickly than thin. First-hand experience will best teach you how to gauge cord length for various designs.

It's much easier and less nerve-wracking to use

your arms to measure off lengths of yarn than to measure it each time with a yardstick. Pick up a length of uncut yarn and hold it loosely at your chest between thumb and forefinger of your left hand. Take the end of it in your other hand and pull it until your right hand and arm are fully extended. The yarn between your chest and outstretched arm is probably about 28 inches long. For a 6-yard cord I'd go through this process about six times and then add two more pulls to make up the difference between me and a yardstick. Violà—you can do the teaberry shuffle or stamp out forest fires while measuring cords. For a very large work you may want to pace off an area of ground and measure by pulling cord over it.

Handling Lengths of Yarn

Controlling long cords is not the problem it might seem to be. Obviously you wouldn't sit close to the floor and attempt to knot with 30-foot cords. In such a case you would work from a ladder or standing on a chair and anchor your dowel as high as comfortable above you. You would do well to work on a section at a time and loop the cords you're not using over a hook or nail or tie them loosely with an overhand or chain knot to move them out of the knotting area. Rubber bands can be used to shorten cords, and, if the yarn is folded upon itself or wrapped over your hand starting close to the knotting, it will feed without difficulty. I find the bundled yarn a handicap in executing most knots, however, and prefer to deal with loose strands, shaking any tangled cords free.

Dealing with Broken Cords

Broken cords or cords that are too short will eventually emerge in one of your works, perhaps because of mismeasurement, faulty spinning, or possibly because a hanging grows into more than what you'd expected. One way to handle the problem is to splice on another length of cord. Certain yarns are easy to splice by separating the plies and simply rolling the two ends together between your fingers. Heavier cords may be more difficult to splice. If the broken cord is receiving knots, as in the knot-bearing cord for clove hitches or the inner strands of a knotted sinnet, you can simply cut the

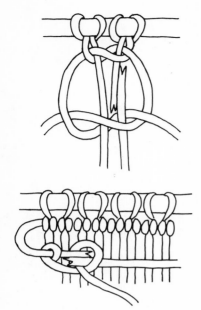

Fig. 3-2 Mending broken knot-receiving cords in a vertical chain of knots (top) and in a row of clove hitches (bottom).

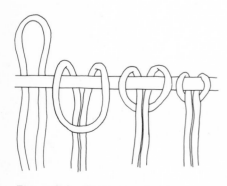

Fig. 3-3 Reverse lark's head.

short cord and lay in a new one about a half an inch from the cut end (fig. 3-2).

Sometimes a cord breaks in the worst possible place and nothing short of a visible glued spot will repair it. Then it's time to bow to misfortune, mutter inaudibly, and realize that you just *knew* a different design should be born. If your work is asymmetrical (it is now!) some fringing or pulling new cords through a heavily knotted area with a weaving needle can give interesting results. Most artists will agree that finding a solution to a medium-created problem is a fantastic learning experience. In any event, you won't soon forget it.

Basic Macrame Knots

Five basic macrame knots are described below: reverse lark's head, square knot, half knot, clove hitch, and diagonal clove hitch. By using these knots in combination with each other, you can create an endless number of designs in macrame work.

Reverse Lark's Head. The reverse lark's head is used to attach cords to the mounting bar or string when beginning a macrame work or to add on additional cords where desired. The loop formed by doubling a cord behind your mounting bar or string is draped over the bar and the ends of the cord are passed through it (fig. 3-3). If you look at the reverse side of this knot, you will see the back of the loop and the knot many people call the lark's head. More people are beginning to use the reverse lark's head for mounting cords to avoid the unnecessary detail of the visible loop.

Square Knot. The square knot is tied, as illustrated in fig. 3-4, by taking the right-hand cord in a group of four, crossing it over the two center filler cords, and placing the left-hand cord over it (a). Then the left-hand cord is brought diagonally up behind the filler cords and through the opening formed by the first cross over (b). When the ends of the knotting cords are evenly pulled, the first half of your square knot will appear (c). To complete your square knot, repeat the directions, but start with the left-hand cord, crossing it over the filler cords and bringing the right cord up on a diagonal and through (d). The completed square knot, shown in

(e) of the illustration, may be tied close to the dowel or previous knot or a distance away from it.

If you have difficulty keeping your filler cords straight while making the square knot, you could tape them or tuck them under the edge of your knotting board to keep them stationary. Sometimes, when making a chain (sinnet) of square knots, you will be interrupted and lose track of which cord you have just used. The small loop indicated by the arrow in (e) will help you determine this. If the loop forms on the right, begin your next knot with the right-hand cord; if it's on the left, begin with the left-hand cord.

Half Knot. The half knot is simply one half of the square knot. To tie it, begin with either the right- or the left-hand cord and create the first part of the square knot, as shown on the top in fig. 3-5. Instead of making a second cross over with the cord on the opposite side, however, continue the procedure beginning from the same side. You'll notice that after a few half knots are tied, the sinnet (chain) begins twisting; toward the right if begun with the left-hand cord, toward the left if begun on the right. To keep the spiral sinnet even, flip the sinnet over after every fourth knot is tied.

Clove Hitch. The clove hitch (also called the double half hitch) is a very versatile knot. With it you can create either free-form or straight lines of knotting. To make a row of horizontal clove hitches, begin, as shown on the top in fig. 3-6, by taking the extreme left-hand cord in a group and pulling it taut *over* all the other cords. This single cord will receive a clove hitch from each of the cords it passes over. It is called the "knot-bearing cord" or "holding cord," because its function is to bear or hold all the knots. Now take the next left-hand cord (your first knotting cord) and pass the end of it over the holding cord and down behind it, remembering to keep the holding cord taut. You have just tied one half hitch. Tighten your loop and repeat the step, looping the end of the knotting cord over the holding cord again and bringing the end through, in front of the first loop, as shown on the bottom in fig. 3-6. This step completes the clove hitch. Tighten your knot, keeping tension on the holding cord, and continue knotting with each succeeding cord.

Diagonal Clove Hitch. This knot is executed in

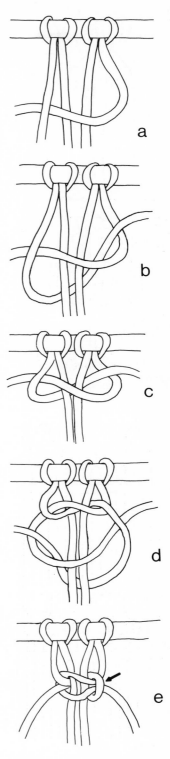

a

b

c

d

e

Fig. 3-4 Square knot.

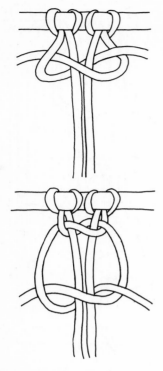

Fig. 3-5   Half knot.

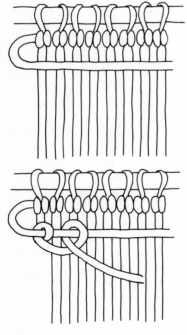

Fig. 3-6   Horizontal clove hitch.

the same way as the clove hitch. It differs only in that the knot-bearing cord is held taut on a diagonal to receive each knot (fig. 3-7). Try clove hitches and diagonal clove hitches using the right-hand cord as the holding cord, directing it toward the left and looping each cord through with your right hand.

Practice the basic macrame knots illustrated before beginning the projects below.

DISCOVERY: "INDIAN BREASTPLATE"

The "Indian Breastplate" hanging shown in fig. 3-8 grew out of experiments with three-sectioned flags, inspired by those of medieval times, and studies of American Indian clothing. The Mohave Indians employed triangular and diamond shapes extensively in their designs and used the color red to represent the sunset or to symbolize thunder.

Although the breastplate shown is meant to be a wall hanging, should you feel enchanted one evening you might consider adding a knotted strap to it and suspending it from your neck. The knots used to create the body of the work are the basic reverse lark's head, half knot, square knot, and clove hitch. Finishing is accomplished with the addition of feathers and wrapping and unplying the yarn ends.

The Heading

To begin, you'll need a 1/4-inch dowel or iron rod 16 inches long and a 1-pound ball of jute. Practice knotting can be done on the small board, but I recommend that you find a place to work while standing for this hanging, as your knotting strands will be quite long at first. As the finished breastplate will be about 30 inches long, and the knotted area is quite dense, each cord should be about 8 yards in length.

Mount thirty 8-yard strands of jute to your dowel using the reverse lark's head knot. Next complete fifteen square knot sinnets (chains), each two knots deep. As each sinnet uses four strands of jute, you will quickly have a heading below your dowel consisting entirely of square knots. This heading is enlarged with another row of square knot sinnets (each two knots deep again), using the two outside strands from each of the previous sinnets to create the row, so that each knot falls inbetween the initial heading of sinnets. (The first and last two cords on the dowel, of course, cannot be used in this row.) Row three of the heading falls in place directly under the first groups of sinnets knotted. In all, seven horizontal rows of double square knots comprise the heading of the breastplate.

The Central Diamond Section

By now you are no doubt tired of dealing with such a mass of cord. But now the hanging becomes divided into three sections, so at this point you can remove the first and last twenty strands of yarn from the knotting area by draping them over nails or tying them off in bundles, leaving the center five sinnets of square knots to work from.

The diamond design (fig. 3-9) is created by knotting multiple rows of horizontal clove hitches. The left center cord of the middle square knot sinnet becomes the first holding or knot-bearing cord for the design. It is held horizontally to the left and all nine cords to the left of it are secured to it with the clove hitch, forming a line directly below the square knots. The next row is accomplished in the same manner, grasping the furthest right of the ten cords for the new holding cord and working toward the left, tying each knot securely and bringing this horizontal row in tightly below the first. As this design calls for closed horizontal clove hitches, the original knot-bearing cord will make the last clove hitch in the second row, leaving no strands exposed and giving a firm edge to the diamond pattern. Continue working toward the left until you have a total of six rows of horizontal clove hitches forming an angled section. You've finished one quarter of the diamond.

For the upper right-hand quarter of the diamond pattern, repeat the above instructions working toward the right, using the remaining center cord below the middle square knot as your knot-bearing cord. Horizontal rows of closed clove hitches complete the top half of the diamond pattern.

The lower half of the diamond is created by using the outermost cord from each angled section as the knot-bearing cord and directing it toward the center of the hanging. By reversing the direction of

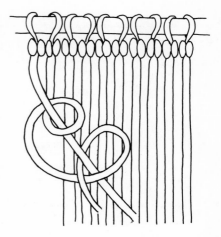

Fig: 3-7   Diagonal clove hitch.

Fig. 3-8 "Indian Breastplate." Rust-red three-ply jute, 15½ x 37 inches.

Fig. 3-9 Central diamond section.

the holding cord and tying another six rows of closed clove hitches, the work is redirected toward the center and the diamond motif is completed.

The size of the diamond in any future work is easily controlled by increasing or decreasing the number of clove hitches on the holding cord and varying the number of horizontal rows completed.

The Central Knotted Section

In the central knotted section (fig. 3-10), the cords extending from the completed central diamond are divided off to echo the sectioned look of the finished hanging. The four outside strands on the left are joined in a half knot sinnet twenty-five knots long which, because it is begun with the right-hand cord, spirals toward the left. The four outside cords on the right are knotted in a similar way, but begun with the left-hand cord which directs the spiral to the right, preserving symmetry in the work. The center twelve cords are joined in single square knots, a row of three knots alternating with a row of two, and ending with a row of three when the knotted area reaches the bottoms of the spiral sinnets.

At this point the single square knots are con-

Fig. 3-10 Central knotted section.

tinued using all twenty cords for five rows. Then the section is divided again to repeat the spirals and square knots (refer to fig. 3-10).

The central section is completed by creating a second large diamond out of horizontal clove hitches, just like the one below the heading.

Remaining Sections

The knotted areas to the left and to the right of the upper central diamond are continuations of the heading. They consist of twenty-four rows of single square knots ending in a repeat of the diamond symbol. Notice that these diamonds are slightly closer to the bottom diamond than they are to the top one. If they were to be centered, the hanging would appear overly symmetrical, and the square formed by the equidistant diamonds would trap the viewer's eye instead of directing it through the total work.

Now tie two sinnets of twenty-five half knots

using the four center cords from the left and the right diamonds.

Wrapping the Rod Tassels

The bulk of the finishing work on the breastplate consists of wrapping a core of jute strands for varying distances, creating smooth fiber cylinders reminiscent of the bonehair pipes used by American Indians in their garments.

The wrapped cords extending from the rod or dowel can be created independently and slipped onto the dowel when completed. A pencil or piece of dowel slightly larger than your hanging rod is useful for holding the cords to be wrapped. Two 24-inch pieces of jute should be cut and draped over the pencil. A strand of jute is then wound around these to create the wrapped cylinder. The wrap consists of coiling a strand of cord around a bundle of yarn, catching itself at first and continuing in neat circles, each new wrap falling in place next to previous one (fig. 3-11). The wrap is ended by using a weaving needle to bring the wrap strand up through the bottom of the coil to secure it. Try to span at least three or more wraps before bringing your needle to the outside of the coil and clipping the wrap strand as close as possible.

I prefer wrapping with a strand of jute which is thinner than the cords used in the body of the hanging, as I feel that this allows a smoother wrapped surface. If you're using a good quality jute, you can get a thin single strand by taking a 2-foot length of it, separating the ply into three strands, and, holding a single strand, pulling the others from it as you would pull a wrapper from a straw. Sometimes it is necessary to roll the jute between your fingers to strengthen a weak spot or to wrap with two strands if your jute is too weak to use a single ply.

Should your wrap strand be too short or should you prefer working with short wrap strands, you can easily absorb the tail of the short wrap strand into the core of cords and continue wrapping with a new strand without any noticeable gap in your work.

Four wrapped tassels extend from the rod; the two outer tassels are 13 inches long, consisting of 4 inches of wrapping and 9 inches of loose jute. The

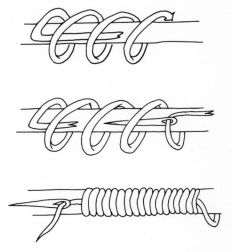

Fig. 3-11 Creating a wrapped tassel.

Fig. 3-12 The completed left diamond section.

inner tassels are 10 inches long and begin with 4½ inches of wrapping.

Wrapping in the Body of the Breastplate

Return to the body of the hanging and join the bottom center diamond by wrapping four strands of jute for 1 inch. Feathers are added by holding them, quill end up, against the core of jute and wrapping over the quills for ½ inch to secure them before ending the wrap. Another wrap is begun below the feathers and continues for 3 inches before a second group of feathers is added and the wrap is ended.

The section below the left diamond (fig. 3-12) consists of, from the left, two loose strands of jute, four strands wrapped for 2½ inches and ending in feathers, another two loose strands of jute, the half knot sinnet, two more loose strands of jute, four strands wrapped for 4½ inches, and another two loose strands. The right diamond is finished in the same way, beginning with the outside and working toward the center.

Trimming and Unplying

The final cutting of a hanging is crucial. It's best to be scissor-shy at first and allow for more length than you believe you'll require. Trim conservatively when you create your own designs, pausing to stand back and evaluate the effects of each new snip. The breastplate is trimmed in steps, echoing the diagonal lines sustained throughout the work. Working from the left, the first eight cords are 12 inches long, and the next twelve cords are 16 inches in length. The center diamond contains four center cords, 20 inches long, flanked by eight cords on either side, each 17 inches in length. The right-hand diamond is trimmed like the left.

Unplying is accomplished by untwisting each cord to separate the ply from each other. Each single cord of three-ply jute can become three strands of jute, and the hanging will grow more full and primitive looking. Although most of the breastplate cords are unplied, I preferred to leave some of the cords intact to add textural interest and to relate back to the wrapped sections. All but a few of the cords extending from the wrapped tassels are left intact and six cords on either side of the center diamond remain whole. The tassels extending from the dowel are totally unplied to counterbalance the wider, lower part of the breastplate.

RELIEF WORK: "AFRICAN SHOVEL MASK—MORANI"

The idea for "Morani" (fig. 3-13; see also color photo 1) was born one afternoon as I walked through the woods growing increasingly irritated by the mosquito-breeding beer cans strewn about collecting water. The shovel blade would have been another piece of garbage but for its beautiful rusted color. As I looked closer, the inverted blade looked back at me, the gentle curves suggesting strongly the planes of a human face. I wished the mosquitoes large families as I headed homeward to begin the fourth in a series of masks. This mask cannot be worn like its precursors, but is unique because it is actually a mask upon a mask. The dark brown neg-

Fig. 3-13 "African Shovel Mask—Morani." 14 x 45 inches.

ative area, showing through the knotted one, becomes the wearer of the fiber face.

Finding a rusted spade should not be difficult. My haunts may be different than yours, but patient persistence will eventually pay off. If all fails or you absolutely cannot wait, get a new blade, apply a metal primer, and paint it brown. It's best to prepare an old blade by wire brushing any loose rust off and washing and drying to remove soil. Then cut any remaining wood flush with the top of the metal.

"Morani" is composed of clove hitches with some wrapping added. More cords are added on after the major part of the mask is completed to give greater dimension and expression to the work. The fibers used in the mask are a natural jute and purple and burgundy wool/cowhair blends. Since the face is composed of two symmetrical halves, you can string only half the work at first and do some of the knotting without the bother of extra cords.

You will also need a wooden or metal ring (mine was a rusted metal one about 2 inches in diameter) and some #18 black annealed wire.

Wiring the Shovel

The knotting is not done directly on the shovel itself, but on a wire attached to the blade. Wiring the blade is more time consuming than difficult. I offer two methods for attaching the wire. The first method is fast and easy and permits you to remove the mask from the shovel to accommodate another one (or perhaps you can think of a better rationalization). The second method is more secure and professional and requires drilling holes in steel, which is a real pain. For those of you who have a drill press or a friend interested in supporting the arts or a conscience like mine, I offer it as an alternate method of wiring.

Method One. This method, illustrated in fig. 3-14, consists of taking a 30-inch length of #18 black annealed wire, forming a 2-inch loop in the middle of it as shown at (a) and guiding either end of it around the sides of the handle or neck and twisting again where the shovel body begins (b). Each piece of wire is then brought just below the top of the blade to the back of the shovel. After stringing your wire, twist the two ends of wire firmly to join them

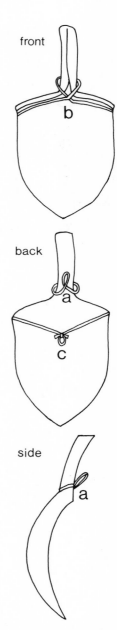

front

back

side

Fig. 3-14 Wiring method one.

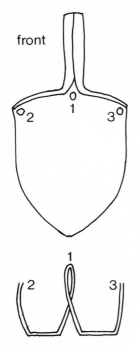

front

Fig. 3-15 Wiring method two.

(c) and temporarily fasten the wires at the neck by taping or wrapping them. The final wrapping of the shovel neck will hold these wires securely and the first loop will function as a hanger for the work.

Method Two This method also uses #18 black annealed wire, but it requires drilling three holes in the blade through which the wire is inserted. You'll need an electric drill, a vise to hold the shovel while drilling, and several $3/32''$ (2.5 mm) drill bits (they dull rapidly during this operation). It would also be helpful to have a hammer and a punch to make an impression for the drilling and a can of household oil to lubricate and cool the bit. If you shorten the bit by scoring the shank (not the cutting end) with a hacksaw and snapping the end off, you'll be able to apply more pressure while drilling without breaking the bit.

Mark the three holes on the blade with a penciled x, in the positions shown on the top in fig. 3-15. The first hole should be on a slight diagonal, boring through any wood that remains in the shovel neck, and should exit the back of the neck about an inch above the shovel body. Holes two and three should be about $1/2$ inch from the edges of the blade. Drill carefully and patiently! When drilling is completed, and any excess oil removed, insert the wire as shown at the bottom in the figure. The back wires can be fastened to each other or secured by wrapping each over a small curved nail behind each hole.

Left Angled Forehead Section

Begin by mounting eight reverse lark's heads, 4 yards each (undoubled length), of natural jute to the left wire on the front of the shovel blade. Working toward the left, the next reverse lark's head is purple wool/cowhair, followed by two of burgundy wool/cowhair. Another single reverse lark's head of purple is followed by a single reverse lark's head of natural again to give an initial working area composed of twenty-six cords. Using the innermost strand as the knot-bearing or holding cord, tie two rows of horizontal clove hitches. At this point, the remaining six right-hand strands of natural jute are cast aside as they will be used later for the vertical forehead band. The angled forehead continues as eight more rows of *closed* horizontal clove hitches are tied. (Remember, closed rows

Fig. 3-16 The right vertical forehead band.

mean that each successive knot-bearing cord is used as the last *knotting* cord in the row beneath it.) After the eight rows are tied toward the left, the knotting direction changes as the last holding cord is directed toward the right. Eight more rows of clove hitches are tied, with each knot-bearing cord directed toward the right. This completes a half-diamond shape.

The Vertical Forehead Bands

Because the wire attached to the shovel slants on a diagonal in this section, the knotting of the forehead band will follow a diagonal, too (fig. 3-16). (Note that the picture shows the *right* vertical band; the diagonals in the *left* vertical band will go in the opposite direction.) The knotting is done with clove hitches, as was the angled forehead section, except that the holding cord is held on a diagonal and hangs free after each row (that is, the holding cord is *not* used to tie the last knot on the subsequent row.) This creates *open* rows of clove hitches. Each

Fig. 3-17 Joining the vertical bands with the half diamond shapes.

of the five rows tied will be shorter than the previous row as the available knotting cords decrease in number. When the five left-directed diagonals on the left forehead band are completed, the first holding cord is held on a right-directed diagonal for another five rows of clove hitches. An additional five rows of left-directed diagonal clove hitches complete this section of the mask.

At this time, if you've been working on one-half the mask, string and knot the right half of the forehead section, reversing directions to preserve symmetry.

Joining the Forehead Sections

The beginning of the elongated nose is formed by joining the vertical forehead bands with the half-diamond shapes. Three more rows of clove hitches are knotted on each band (they can be seen at the bottom of the band in fig. 3-16). Then the holding cord from the last row of knots on the half-diamond section is used as the holding cord for another open row of knots on the vertical band. This connects the two sections. Now another open row of clove hitches is tied toward the center all the way across the bottom of the half-diamond shape and the vertical band. Figure 3-17 shows the half-diamond joined to the left vertical band, but not yet joined to the right band.

It is advisable now, because of the number of cords in the working area, to tie them off in sections. Starting from the outside edges, ten colored and natural strands can be bundled; they will later become the cheeks. Separate the next ten strands on each side into groups of five; these will become the outsides and the insides of each eye. Remaining are two sets of cords extending from each vertical band waiting to be joined.

Fig. 3-18 Joining the vertical bands to begin the nose.

Beginning the Nose

Pull the two vertical forehead bands together until the uppermost holding cords touch. The top holding cord from the right vertical band should be held on a left-directed diagonal to receive the five cords extending from the left side of the mask (fig. 3-18). This row of clove hitches will join the two sections and begin the nose of the mask. The uppermost cord that is used to make the first clove hitch in this diagonal row becomes the knot-bearing cord for the four remaining cords on the right side of the mask. A second row of closed clove hitches is done on each side of the nose before laying these cords aside to begin work on the eyes.

The Eyes

Undo the bundles of five cords that hang down from the bottom of each half diamond. Each group of five cords, which become either side of the eyes, are knotted on a diagonal as illustrated in fig. 3-19. Two closed rows of diagonal clove hitches are formed, followed by four open rows. If you bend the knotted area gently to form a curve, the two sections of the eye can be easily joined in a single clove hitch, causing the macrame to protrude slightly.

Joining the Nose and Eyes

Returning to the nose, continue the diagonal rows of clove hitches, incorporating the cords from the inner eye sections into the work. Nine open rows of clove hitches are tied, connecting the inner eye sections to the nose pieces. In fig. 3-19, three of the nine rows have been made. When all nine are completed, the top three cords should be separated off as they will become part of the lower cheek. The remaining cords are knotted with the open rows of clove hitches directed diagonally toward the center of the shovel. Direction changes again as two diagonal rows of closed clove hitches are directed toward the outside of the shovel, followed by three more open rows. These rows of knots are visible in the vertical band just to the right of center in fig. 3-20. One-half inch of wrapping (I used the burgundy wool for this) binds the ends of the nose pieces, which can now be clipped to become 2-inch tufts, clearing the knotting area.

The Lower Cheek

The lower cheek is made by knotting the five cords extending from the outer eye area along with the three cords separated off from the nose. Use the outermost cord from the eye as your first holding cord and make diagonal rows of open clove hitches directed toward the shovel center. The lower cheeks completed to this point can be seen on the left and right in fig. 3-20, below the outer eye sections. Then reverse direction and knot toward the outside of the shovel; change direction again and knot toward the center.

The Upper Cheek

The remaining unknotted cords extending from the half-diamond angled forehead sections are knotted in open rows of outward-directed horizontal clove hitches. These are followed by open rows

Fig. 3-19   Joining the nose and eye sections.

Fig. 3-20   The nose and lower cheek sections.

Fig. 3-21   The completed upper cheek and headdress.

Fig. 3-22   Beginning of the headdress.

of verticle clove hitches formed when the knot-bearing cord is directed downward toward the point of the shovel blade (see fig. 3-21). Your first holding cord in this vertically-knotted section is the same one used as the first holding cord in the outward-directed horizontal rows. The upper cheek section is completed by tying two outward-directed closed rows of horizontal clove hitches. Notice in this cheek section how color disappears and reappears as the colored cords serve first as holding cords and then as knotting cords.

The Headdress

Four new cords are added just below the outside tip of the half-diamond forehead section to create a headdress-like extension of the mask. The back side of the clove hitched work consists of loops of jute, perfect for accepting new strands. Cut four cords, 3 yards each, and use a weaving needle to pull them halfway through four separate loops at the back of the forehead section. They should be close to the edge of the knotted area and equidistant from each other. You will end up with eight working cords (see fig. 3-22).

Knot the eight new cords, beginning with an inward-directed diagonal, in six closed rows of clove hitches. After the sixth row is tied, the last holding cord reverses direction to begin another six closed rows of knots. Turning your shovel blade will facilitate knotting in this awkward direction. Notice how the angle formed relates back to the forehead angles. After the sixth row, the cords are separated into two groups to be knotted in closed inward-directed rows of diagonal clove hitches. The first band contains twenty rows of knots; the second contains ten. The completed headdress can be seen in fig. 3-21.

Mouth and Nose Attachment

I've used a 2-inch-diameter rusted metal ring to suggest the mouth in the mask illustrated, but any size or type ring can be employed. The two nose sections are joined, midway down, with a piece of yarn connecting two loops in the reverse side of the work. The tufted nostril extensions are then inserted through the ring, entering from the front, and pulled upward and outward to be fastened to

Fig. 3-23 The attached mouth ring and completed nose and beard.

the lower cheek dressings with a stitch in the back of the work. The mouth ring is now held in place by the fastened nostrils (see fig. 3-23).

The Beard

The beard is formed by covering the bottom of the mouth ring with ten reverse lark's heads resulting in twenty strands of jute. The two centermost lark's heads are formed with two jute cords each 3 yards long. The remaining lark's heads are tied with cords 1½ yards in length. A single row of clove hitches is begun on either side of the ring and is directed toward the center of the ring to end just before reaching the long center cords. The two sets of four outside cords receive fifteen closed rows of center-directed diagonal clove hitches, and the center four cords (the long ones) receive thirty closed rows of left-directed diagonal clove hitches (fig. 3-23).

Wrapping the Handle

The shovel handle is wrapped at this time, forming a head decoration for the mask. Consisting of natural jute with two stripes of colored wool/cowhair added midway through, the wrapping is begun at the base of the handle and ends at a point about 1/2 inch from the top. Place the stripes where you choose, using as many as you like, and adding new wrap cords by simply covering up the end of the old one with the new. (How to wrap is described under Wrapping the Rod Tassels in the "Indian Breastplate" project, and is illustrated in fig. 3-11.) I have added a band of clove hitches at the base of the handle wrapping over the top ends and tucking the lower ones under the wire (see fig. 3-13). Alternatives are to add unplied jute or feathers or to leave the area exposed.

Trimming

Cut the jute and wool extending from the mask cautiously, either approximating the proportions of the one illustrated in fig. 3-13 (the longest fringe is about 25 inches) or in a manner pleasing to you. The drama of the work changes radically with the length of cord remaining. Unply the jute ends and "Morani" is completed.

SCULPTURE: "COCOON"

The fact that insects love to build their nests and hives under the eaves of newly erected houses was not known to me when I began my career as a house painter. (One can support a fiber habit in a variety of ways.) I didn't love the buzzing critters flying around my head and scolding me from my ladder jack, but I did enjoy seeing the various cocoon and hive structures the insects built and have used many of their designs in my fiberwork. The potter wasp's nest which inspired "Cocoon" (fig. 3-24) was so incredible that I must admit—you've already guessed—I painted around it! I have recently discovered an amazing book called *Insects of the World* by Walter Linsenmaier in which you can see an astounding assortment of structures created by our natural artisans without the risk of getting stung.

Fig. 3-24 "Cocoon." 6 x 9 inches.

"Cocoon" is made with either jute or sisal and is composed of clove hitches with some wrapping added. Various colors of narrow three-ply jute are used to create the surface details. The highly textured appearance of the large cone is due to the fact that the reverse side of the clove hitch is visible in this work. The neat rows of knots used in the previous macrame projects are on the inside of the cocoon.

Beginning the Cocoon

This work is mounted on an 8-inch-diameter metal ring which gives firm support to the first row of knots but is not visible in the finished work. Begin by stringing 3-yard-long heavy jute or sisal cords to the ring, attaching with the reverse lark's head and continuing until the ring is covered. The last lark's head should be formed with a 12-yard-long cord; $4^1/_2$ feet of cord should extend from one side of the lark's head and $10^1/_2$ yards should extend from the other. The long cord will be the holding or knot-bearing cord throughout this work. It will circle and climb atop each previous row to form the cone shape.

It will be much easier to work on this piece if you immobilize the base ring. I found that tying the ring to a knotting board, as illustrated in fig. 3-25, worked very well. Thin cotton string should be used so that after the cone is completed you can cut the string and easily pull it through the knotted work.

The First Row of Clove Hitches

Begin your first row of clove hitches outside the lark's heads as shown in fig. 3-26, working either in a clockwise or a counter-clockwise direction, whichever seems easier for you. Use the $10^1/_2$-yard cord as your holding cord. As you knot around the outside of the ring, the cords should be pulled away from the center of the circle. When the next rows of clove hitches are knotted above the first, the looped pattern characteristic of the back side of clove hitches will begin to appear on the outside of the cocoon. (If you were to direct your lark's heads toward the inside of the ring and pull each clove hitch toward the inside, a normal clove hitch pattern would appear on the outside of your cocoon.)

Building the Cone Shape

Knot two rows of clove hitches. For row three, omit every fourth cord by cutting it to an 8-inch length and placing the end in the center of the ring. By decreasing the number of knotting cords, you can cause the cocoon walls to taper inward. Remember to place your holding cord on top of each knotted row or you will create a flat circle instead of a three-dimensional shape.

Knot a fourth row of clove hitches using the same number of cords as in row three. Then, on the fifth row, skip every sixth cord, tapering again. (Remember to trim the skipped cords and place the ends in the center of the cocoon.) Row six is knotted using all the cords used in row five. In knotting row seven, skip every sixth cord. What you have before you now is a bottomless basket full of jute strands. You could stop right here and call the piece "Diet of Worms"—or else continue to clove hitch rows eight and nine. In row ten, skip every fourth strand, and then knot three more rows. This completes the cocoon.

Finishing the Cocoon Opening

The jute ends at the top of the knotted structure can be cut and unplied or else pulled to the center

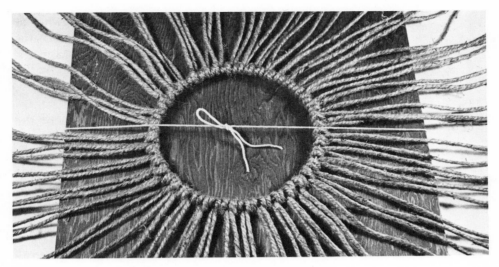

Fig. 3-25 The covered ring attached to a working surface.

Fig. 3-26 Beginning the first row of clove hitches.

Fig. 3-27 Cords mounted to begin a small projecting cocoon.

of the cone in a bundle, as in the work shown. Use whatever idea you prefer, but leave a few of the strands free as they will be wrapped to form the vinelike surface details.

The Small Projecting Cocoons

The loops forming the outside surface of the large cocoon are perfect for receiving new cords with which you can create other tiny projecting cocoons. If the cords used to create these are made of narrow three-ply jute, they can be easily threaded through a weaving needle and carried under the loops. Mount the cords so they outline a circular or oval shape, as shown in fig. 3-27. Each cord should be about 1 foot long, forming two 6-inch-long strands that extend from either side of the loop when strung. As a holding cord is required once again, cut one cord to a $3^1/_2$-foot length and let one end of it extend for about 3 feet.

Make your small cocoon the same way you created the large one, omitting cords to get tapered walls or using all the cords to bring the cocoon walls straight up. Jute ends can be carried to the inside of the work with a weaving needle, or they can be cut and unplied to finish off the small cocoon openings. Try creating some of these projections with the normal clove hitch pattern on the outside of the work and then try forming one small cocoon with another engulfing it. Experiment freely here—you can easily remove any small cocoons you don't like.

The Wrapped Vines

Some of the heavy jute cords at the lip of the large cocoon can be wrapped and snaked between the small cocoons to give more detail to the work. Begin wrapping at the top of the work, and when the vine is the desired length, end the wrap and pull the end of the jute cord back into the large cone.

Experiment with other clove hitched structures, building forms with walls that climb straight up or grow outward. You can then assemble these to form a larger piece of sculpture, representing perhaps the nest groupings of the mud wasp, or depicting an idea of your own.

WRAPPING

In addition to being used as a finishing technique for other fiber media, wrapping can be employed alone to create fiber works. It is the same process described in the chapter on macrame (see fig. 3-11 and accompanying text) and consists of covering a core material (or warp) with consecutive wraps, using a strand of yarn called the weft or wrapping strand.

TOOLS AND WORKING METHODS

The tools needed for wrapping (fig. 4-1) are needles for carrying the weft strand back into the core to end the wrap, alligator clips to hold weft strands before securing them, and some lightweight wire to be added to the core when a firm support is

Fig. 4-1 Wrapping supplies.

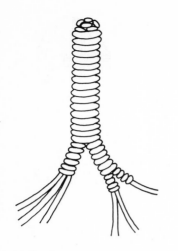

Fig. 4-2 Branching a wrapped core.

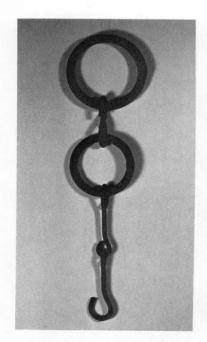

Fig. 4-3 The rusted rings which form the basis for the design.

needed. The wire is important in a work containing multiple symmetrical curves, especially if the core or warp is composed of a soft material. When forming a long continuous wrap, rubber bands may be used to bundle lengths of yarn and shorten the wrapping strand.

By dividing the warp strands extending from a wrapped section, one can create additional, smaller wrapped branches from it (fig. 4-2). Also, cords may be added or subtracted during the wrapping process to create thick or thin tubelike structures, and already wrapped cords may be bundled together to create even thicker wrapped areas. Designs may be formed using various colored yarns in the weft, and grasses, feathers, or even driftwood may be wrapped into the piece to give added detail.

One advantage to creating wrapped pieces is that, because they are linear, ideas can be easily sketched before executing them. This is particularly valuable in a piece like "Indian Tomb" in which proportions are so important and the amount of trimming is crucial to the work.

As the wrapping procedure is not complex, an examination of the three works described below, each of which employ a found object, should guide you in designing your own wrapped fiber pieces. To gain even better practice in designing your own wrapped works, visit a hardware store or a junk shop to find a wooden or metal object to work from. Then draw the found object a few times on separate sheets of paper and on each drawing sketch a different idea for a wrapped fiberwork. Your designs can echo or depart from the design of the found object. Because a simple line represents the wrapped cords quite well, your drawing ability won't influence your success in completing this task. (Straight lines can get pretty boring anyway.) For example, alternate designs using the same double rings employed in "Indian Tomb" are illustrated in fig. 4-4.

DISCOVERY: "INDIAN TOMB"

Two iron rings joined by an S-hook (fig. 4-3) form the basis for the design of this wrapped hanging (fig. 4-5). Old rusted rings may be joined to create a similar base for your work, or new rings and hooks may be purchased from a hardware store, primed, and then painted brown. For yarn I used a dark brown cable cord (cotton seine) that blended with the rusted metal so that the fiber might become an extension of the metal objects, which are themselves visually pleasing. The cord is attached to the rings by draping it over rather than by tying it on with lark's head knots, as this would create extra bulk and ruin the start of the smooth wrapped sections. The fiber covers the rings only where the wrapped cords meet the rings; otherwise the metal is exposed.

The Top Ring Extensions

Two wrapped tubes, each containing an eight-strand warp, curve inward from the top ring before meeting the bottom of the ring. Four strands of each core pass on either side of the metal. Then the wrapping continues in outward curves to meet the lower ring. Again the core is split to pass around the metal and the wrapping is continued in half-circle shapes within the ring. After reattaching to the metal, another 2 inches of wrapping below the ring completes these extensions. The cord used in this piece is rigid enough to support these short curves, but wire could be added as part of the warp if a softer yarn were employed. A twelve-strand wrapped tube extends from each side of the top ring. These tubes separate into three branches as illustrated (the side branches are slightly longer than the center one) before being reunited into a main trunk. The wrap strands on two of the three branches must be secured with clips to prevent unraveling, while the wrap strand from the third branch continues to join the reunited cords. This part of the work is now temporarily secured by using alligator clips or by ending the wrap (bringing the end back under the last few wraps with a weaving needle) before beginning work on the lower ring.

The Lower Ring Extensions

The extensions on either side of the lower ring contain a core of eight strands of cotton seine wrapped as one tube for a short distance before separating into two branches. They are reunited and then joined with the top ring side extensions to end in a wrapped trunk containing twenty strands

Fig. 4-4 Different designs using the same ring base as in "Indian Tomb."

Fig. 4-5 "Indian Tomb." 18 x 43 inches.

Fig. 4-6 "Vixen's Earth." #24 and #36 white cotton seine, 14 x 56 inches.

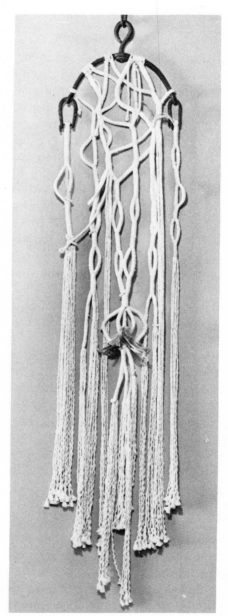

of cotton cord and some feathers for accent. The metal hook extending from the lower ring contains two tassels, each wrapped for a short distance. One contains feathers; the other, long thin wrapped pieces which are created independently and attached to the main tassel by drawing a warp cord from each thin wrapped piece underneath the wrapping on the tassel.

Trimming

The trimming of a linear piece such as this one should be done carefully and unplying kept to a minimum to avoid softening such an explicit statement.

RELIEF WORK: "VIXEN'S EARTH"

"Vixen's Earth" (fig. 4-6) is a wrapped hanging of cotton seine mounted on a curved piece of iron found at a flea market. The found object becomes part of the hanging, but, unlike "Indian Tomb," does not dictate the design of the work. "Vixen's Earth" is one in a series of hangings called "Travels with a Downed Bird," and it represents the network of tunnels a female fox or vixen had made as part of her underground home. Some wrapped paths lead nowhere, representing those created to foil intruders, while others lead directly to the center of the hanging, the vixen's den. The feathers represent parts of the dead bird the fox has dropped on her way through the tunnels.

Design Elements

Although it appears much more complicated, the techniques employed in this hanging are variations of the same processes used to create "Indian Tomb." Your own design will depend somewhat on the shape of the found-object base you have selected to use, but the techniques and elements of design will be the same: wrapping tubes of various thicknesses and lengths; joining, separating, and rejoining branches; judiciously adding design details such as feathers and tassels; contrasting wrapped and unwrapped areas; trimming carefully, etc. Although "Vixen's Earth" is entirely of white cotton, you may want to use color accents as part of your design. You will undoubtedly want to

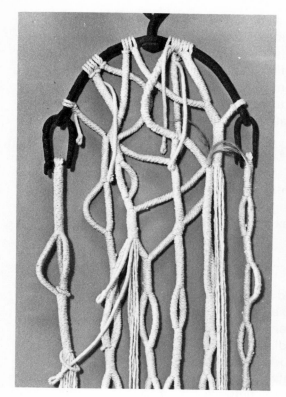

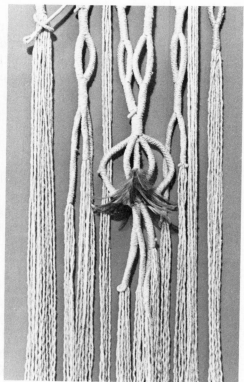

Fig. 4-7   Upper half of "Vixen's Earth."   Fig. 4-8   Lower half of "Vixen's Earth."

sketch your idea before you begin, but may find yourself altering it slightly as it grows on you.

Textural Details

One of the most important textural features of "Vixen's Earth" is the cotton seine itself—its uneven thickness contributes greatly to the textural interest of the work.

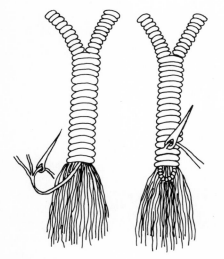

Fig. 4-9   Creating the wormlike loops.

The small wormlike loops attached to some of the wrapped branches give the work further detail (see figs. 4-7 and 4-8). The loops are created by first taking one of the three-ply core yarns and threading a single ply of it through a needle, as seen on the left in fig. 4-9. This single ply of yarn is then pulled rapidly back into a wrapped section, and a natural coil results as the other plies are moved away from the threaded one. Any plies not caught in the wrap by this process can be pulled through independently with the needle. Finally, "Vixen's Earth" contains areas of unplied yarn not only at the end of the work, but in the body of the hanging

Fig. 4-10 "Secret Garden." 6 x 56 inches.

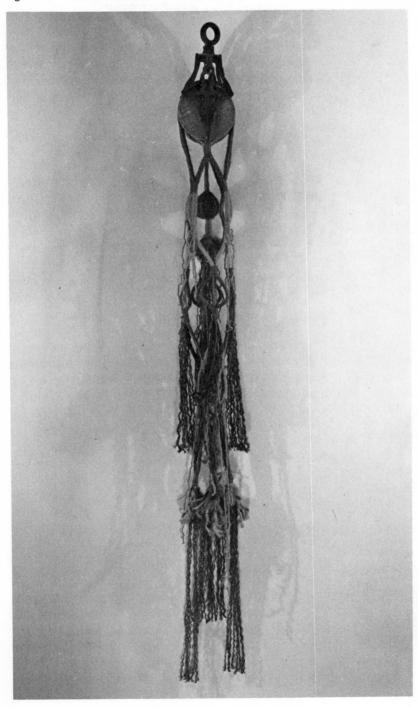

as well. These are present to add textural and visual contrast and prevent the viewer's eye from becoming trapped in a maze of smoothly wrapped trunks and branches.

SCULPTURE: "SECRET GARDEN"

"Secret Garden" (fig. 4-10) was inspired by cave stalactites and images of the hanging gardens of antiquity. The antique pulley from which "Secret Garden" hangs did not originally inspire this work, but it seemed the perfect complement to the garden idea and the preliminary drawings of the piece. When I realized how well the ornate ironwork would echo the wrapped structure and how naturally the pulley would receive the warp cords, I knew I'd found the ideal supporting structure. Although the wood and iron of an old tool add to the piece, a painted metal pulley obtained from a hardware store could also serve in this work.

The warp cords in "Secret Garden" are heavy jute, wrapped with various shades of blue and green wool. Rooster feathers and dark green jute are incorporated into the design at several points.

The Pod

The podlike sphere suspended in the center of the work is created first, and the outer structure is composed around it. The sphere is actually a 2¹/₂-inch-diameter wooden ball, obtained from a lumber yard, with a 1-inch hole drilled through it. Olive green wool yarn is wrapped over the ball, as illustrated in fig. 4-11, until all the wood is concealed. Then the yarn ends are pulled tightly into the wrapping to secure them.

The Pod Vine

Suspending the pulley from a ceiling or door jam hook or tying it to a ceiling fixture or tree branch will make the execution of this work considerably easier. To create the vine which holds the pod, drape a 3-foot length of heavy jute over the pulley wheel to extend for about 16 inches on either side of it. Then grasp the two jute cords just below the pulley and join them by wrapping with slate blue wool for about 3 inches. Now add about ten 2-foot strands of olive yarn to the warp core and continue the wrap for another inch. At this point, separate

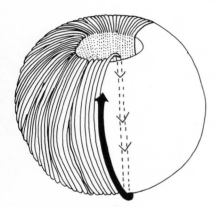

Fig. 4-11 Wrapping the ball which forms the pod.

Fig. 4-12 Encircling the ball with the pod vine.

the jute into two branches, leaving the wool strands free, and wrap each jute cord for several inches or until the two wrapped branches can encircle the pod. Arrange the wrapped jute cords and the wool strands around the pod, pull them tightly around it, and join them underneath the pod by wrapping again for 1½ inches, adding rooster feathers before ending the wrap (fig. 4-12). The jute cord is clipped just below the end of the wrapping, so that only the lengths of wool yarn extending from the pod vine are visible.

Wrapping and Stringing the Pulley Cords

Four 10-foot-long heavy jute cords are partially wrapped with slate blue wool and then strung on the pulley, resulting in eight lengths of cord which, when wrapped, joined, and separated, create the vine network. To wrap and string these pulley cords, first take two of the jute cords, place them next to each other, and wrap them together for the middle 12 inches of the 4-foot length with slate blue wool. Then separate the cords and wrap each of the four branches for 2½ inches, as illustrated in fig. 4-13. Drape these cords halfway over the pulley wheel.

The two remaining 10-foot cords are wrapped individually with the same slate blue wool for the middle 8 inches of their length. Now place one of these cords on each side of the pulley, over the ironwork, resting between it and the pulley wheel. Join the two cord halves on each side of the pulley with a 1-inch wrap, then separate the cords and wrap each branch for 2½ inches, as seen in fig. 4-14.

Joining the Cords in V Shapes

The eight cords extending from the pulley are now joined to each other, forming four V-shaped designs. The cords are joined with a 1½-inch wrap of the slate blue wool (see fig. 4-14).

The First Oval Shapes

The first oval shapes are created by wrapping each of the two cords extending from the Vs with apple green wool for 3 inches, then rejoining them by wrapping for 1 inch (fig. 4-15). Instead of wrapping over any short weft ends, I have let them extend,

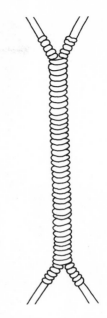

Fig. 4-13 Two of the wrapped pulley cords.

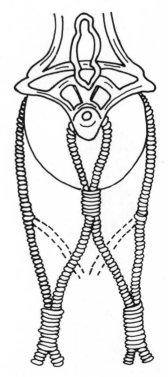

Fig. 4-14 The wrapped and mounted pulley cords and the first V-shapes.

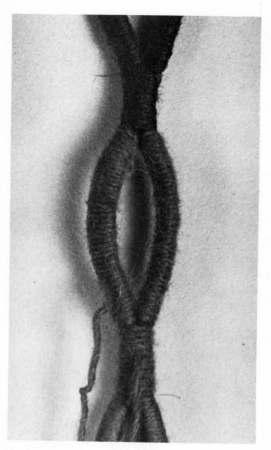

Fig. 4-15 The first oval shape.

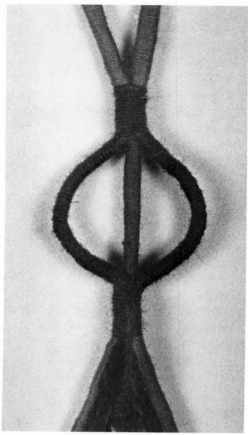

Fig. 4-16 The second V and three-part oval.

throughout this work, as part of the design. (You can see two of them in fig. 4-15.) First I pulled the ends back under a couple of wraps, thereby fastening each wrapped area before beginning with a new cord, but then let the tail hang untrimmed. You can absorb these weft ends into the wrap, if you like, or add hanging ends by pulling single strands of wool into the finished wrapped areas.

The Second Vs and Three-Part Ovals

To make the second V-shaped section, wrap each cord extending from the first oval in light blue wool for 3 inches. Then join each cord with its adjacent partner cord and four additional 1-foot strands of dark green jute. Wrap the two cords and the four pieces of jute together for 1 inch with olive green wool (fig. 4-16). The three branches in the ovals which follow are created by wrapping over the added jute with a grey-green wool for 2$\frac{1}{2}$ inches and wrapping over each of the primary jute cords for a distance of 3$\frac{1}{2}$ inches. When all three wrapped cords are joined again in an olive green 1-inch wrap, the two side cords will curve and project in the wide oval shapes (see fig. 4-16).

The Third Vs and Ovals

Each primary jute cord extending from the three-part ovals is now wrapped with light blue wool for 4 inches before being joined with its neighbor as in the first V, and then separated and rejoined with apple green wool as in the first oval. The added green jute that extends from the three-part oval hangs, unplied, in 6- and 10-inch lengths, adding fullness to the work and echoing the loose cords extending from the pod vine. The loose jute and the beginning of the third V can be seen at the bottom of fig. 4-16.

Completion

The two cords forming each of the final ovals are wrapped together with slate blue wool for 1 inch. Then they are separated and each cord is wrapped for 6 inches with the same blue wool. These cords are then joined in Vs with a 1-inch wrap which incorporates rooster feathers and four 1-foot pieces of green jute. Finally, the eight main jute cords are clipped to 3-inch lengths and all extending cords are unplied, giving fullness to the bottom of the hanging.

The moving shadows cast by "Secret Garden" as it slowly turns are really beautiful to see. Place the work in sunlight, near trailing plants if possible; my Swedish Ivy climbs in and out of the wrapped sections, forming another garden within this one.

COILING

TOOLS AND WORKING METHODS

Coiling is a fiber technique consisting of wrapping yarn around a core material and winding the resulting coil into the desired shape. The coils are held in place by stitches taken after every few wraps. The only tools you'll need to create baskets or fiberworks with coiling are some large-eyed tapestry needles and a pair of scissors. Optional supplies are wire, which can be used to support soft core materials or wrapped protrusions, and modeling clay, which you can use to form a coiled model of a piece before executing it in yarn.

Choosing and Measuring the Warp

In coiling, the core material, also called the warp, functions like the holding cord in macrame. It receives the wrapping material, or weft, and serves as a support and shaping mechanism for the piece. The diameter and rigidity of the warp will determine the size and stability of your finished work. Obviously three coils of human hair can't compare with three coils of garden hose (check it out!). I usually use heavy 1/4-inch-diameter three-ply jute as a warp material, but sisal, rope, leather, cotton clothes line, or paper rush also work well.

As the core does no wrapping itself, it's fairly easy to estimate how long a piece you'll need for a specific work. As always, it's wise to overestimate until you get a feel for the medium. (If you underestimate, however, you *can* add more warp. See Adding Weft and Warp, below.)

Choosing a Weft

A wrapping or weft material thin enough to fit through the eye of a weaving needle and sturdy enough to withstand the stress of wrapping and fastening will be most convenient for coiling. A thick weft, however, can be used with a makeshift needle created from a piece of wire.

Fig. 5-1   Coiling supplies.

Beginning a Coil

To start a coil you'll need a 3-foot section of weft yarn and a length of warp yarn cut at a slant so it's tapered at one end. Thread the weft yarn through a needle, and, starting about 2 inches from the tapered end of the warp, wrap toward the other end of the warp for about 1½ inches (fig. 5-2, top and middle). Then bend the wrapped section back to form a loop and continue wrapping, covering the raw edge of the doubled core yarn and securing the tail of the coil to the loop with a figure-8 stitch (fig. 5-2, bottom).

Basic Coiling Stitches

Figure-8 Stitch. This stitch, which is one method of attaching adjacent wrapped coils to each other, is worked between the coils. The weaving needle, threaded with the weft yarn, is brought around the outside of the warp, inserted in between the coils, around the bottom coil and once again between the coils (fig. 5-3). The wrapping process is then continued for five or six more turns and another figure-

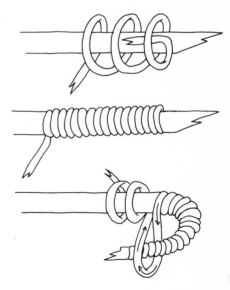

Fig. 5-2   Beginning the coil.

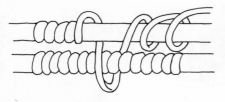

Fig. 5-3   Figure-8 stitch.

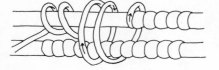

Fig. 5-4   Line stitch.

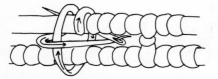

Fig. 5-5   Lace stitch.

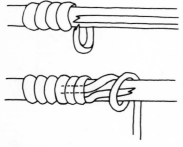

Fig. 5-6   Adding a weft or wrapping cord.

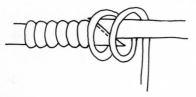

Fig. 5-7   Adding a warp cord.

8 stitch is taken. The stitch follows a figure-8 or s-curve, and when done correctly it is almost invisible against the weft.

Lazy Squaw or Line Stitch. An alternate method of attaching coils is the lazy squaw (I find the term offensive and prefer to call it the line stitch). The line stitch is formed by wrapping two coils with one stitch, forming a visible vertical line which adds detail to the work (fig. 5-4). It's best to do the line stitch twice before continuing the wrap, as this is a weaker method of attaching the coils.

Lace Stitch. The lace stitch consists of adding one or several knots to the line stitch (fig. 5-5). It serves as decoration by itself and by creating a space between the coils.

Adding Weft and Warp Cords

If weft cords were longer than the recommended 3 feet they would be difficult to handle. As coiling consumes cord rapidly, however, new weft yarns must be added frequently. To accomplish this, simply lay on a new weft, considering it part of the core, and wrap over it a few times (fig. 5-6). Then cut and drop the old weft and begin wrapping with the new one, catching the end of the discarded weft in the first few wraps.

Warp can be added on if necessary by tapering the ends of the old and new warps and carefully wrapping over both warp ends at their joint before continuing with the wrap (fig. 5-7).

Ending the Coil

Coiling is ended in the same way as is wrapping: a needle carries the weft end back inside the coil to exit five or six wraps back into the work. The weft end can be trimmed close to the wrapping. The warp cord may extend, unplied, as part of the design, or it may be cut, tapered, wrapped and attached to the coil below it before being needle-woven back under the last few wraps. (See fig. 5-8.)

DISCOVERY: "CEREMONIAL MAT"

"Ceremonial Mat" (fig. 5-9 and color photo 3) is inspired by an Ethiopian straw mat which hangs on my kitchen chimney. The warp for this piece is about 8 feet long, and the coils are joined by figure-8 stitches. The wrapped tassels are added on after coiling is completed. I used green, white, and yellow wool yarns, and a white cowhair/wool blend for the tassels.

The Center Star

The center of the mat, a series of green wool-wrapped coils, is 2 inches in diameter, and the coils comprising it are joined with the figure-8 about every six wraps. Halfway around the fifth coil a weft of white wool is added. From that point on, four wraps of white wool alternate with four wraps of green wool, creating the beginnings of the star points. The green weft is carried along the core as white is wrapped over it, and then the white weft is carried as the green is used (see fig. 5-10). This eliminates the need for laying on new cords each time a color is changed. Make your figure-8 stitches only where you are joining same-colored sections of wrapped coil. The next (sixth) coil consists of six wraps of white, alternating with two of green. This completes the star points.

Notice in fig. 5-9 how the coiling process prevents the design from being totally symmetrical. Artisans in many cultures often deliberately break the symmetry of an otherwise mirror-image piece because to attempt perfection is considered an affront to their gods. An authentic oriental carpet can become a playground as you search for the inevitable flaw—great fun at some otherwise boring cocktail parties.

Completing the Mat

Two coils of solid white wool continue the work as the green weft, no longer needed, is cut and absorbed as part of the warp. At the end of the second white coil, midway between two green star points, a yellow weft is added and a yellow triangle is begun. Two wraps of yellow are followed by about ten of white as each new yellow point is placed between the green ones.

The next coil contains four wraps of yellow, centered above the first two, alternating with wraps of white. This completes the yellow triangles. When this is done, drop the white weft and add one coil of solid yellow to finish the mat.

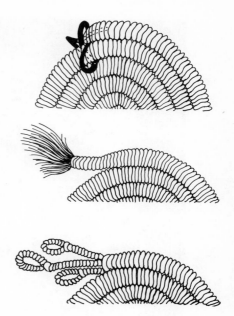

Fig. 5-8 Three methods of ending a coil: tapering and attaching (top), unplying (middle), and wrapping divided ply (bottom).

Fig. 5-9 "Ceremonial Mat."
5½-inch diameter.

Tassels

As the figure-8 stitch could only be employed in the triangle areas, the final yellow coil is less securely attached than the previous ones. The resulting open spaces between the stiches can be used to accommodate yarn which, when wrapped, forms the finish detail in the mat. Twenty symmetrically spaced tassels of white cowhair/wool yarn, wrapped in yellow, green, and white wool, complete the mat. The ten smallest wrapped pieces are pulled forward to create depth, and the naturally kinked cowhair/wool fringe is trimmed evenly around the mat. The work could be trimmed in a variety of other ways: by the addition of feathers, bells, or smaller coiled pieces, or by unplying the fringe to various lengths.

RELIEF WORK:
"SOMEWHERE THE SUN SHINES"

This small wrapped and coiled piece (fig. 5-11) is part of a series I call "Sky Forms." Its abstract sim-

Fig. 5-10 The center star
with added white weft.

plicity is sustained with muted changes in color
(off-white, slate blue, and grey-green) almost hid-
ing the small bursts of yellow-orange that are re-
cessed from the coiled surface. The piece is
created in two separate sections, joined with the
figure-8 stitch.

Rainbow Section

The four rainbow-like curved pieces at the top of
the work are wrapped individually and joined
together and shaped after the smallest is completed (fig. 5-12). The core of warp material consists of multiple strands of grey-green wool along
with a thin piece of wire to help create the curved
form. The outermost coil is begun on a bundle of
38-inch-long strands of yarn. The wrapped part is
10 inches long, and the wrapping begins 14 inches
from the end of the bundle. Three inches of off-
white wrapping is followed by $2^1/2$ inches of slate
blue, then by $1^1/2$ inches of grey-green and another
3 inches of off-white. Each succeeding wrapped
tube becomes progressively smaller, and the blue
begins and the green ends at points $1/2$ inch from
the previous wrapped section to create the pattern
seen in fig. 5-12.

Fig. 5-11 ''Somewhere the Sun Shines.'' 6 x 19 inches.

Fig. 5-12 The rainbow section.

Fig. 5-13 The center relief section.

A strand of off-white yarn should extend from each end of the smallest coil to be used in a figure-8 stitch, joining the four single tubes in the white areas of the work. The blue and green sections will be secured later with a separate strand of green wool extending from the center relief section of the hanging. If necessary, additional stitching may be done on the reverse side of the work or through the center of the coils to hold them securely.

Center Relief Section

The center coiled work on this hanging (fig. 5-13) is formed on a bundle of 50-inch-long grey-green warp cords. First an inverted basket shape is made, using the same technique used to create "Ceremonial Mat," except that here the first three coils are placed almost on top of each other, instead of beside each other. The coils are wrapped with grey-green wool and joined with the figure-8 stitch. Two flat coils continue this section. The third flat coil departs from the circular design to establish an oval structure. On the third flat coil, just after a joining stitch, wrap continuously for twenty-five turns and bend this wrapped tube to create a gap between it and the lower coil, before reattaching it to the work. The bent coil will look like a small handle. This process should be repeated when you reach a point directly opposite the first detached coil. The next foil follows the shape created by these handlelike protrusions and ends in the center of the second detached coil. The last weft thread is carried back through the coil to secure the wrapping, while the warp cords are left exposed as part of the design.

Joining and Finishing the Sections

Bright yellow-orange embroidery threads, used to represent the sun, are added to the center relief section by stitching back and forth behind the openings at the "handles," attaching the threads to the reverse side of the work. The two sections are joined using a strand of grey-green wool and one of the stitches described earlier. Finally, the cords are trimmed on a curve, with the longest strands on the outside, echoing the curved look of the initial rainbow shape. A small loop of yarn is added to the back of the work to facilitate hanging.

SCULPTURE: "LICHEN BED"

"Lichen Bed" (fig. 5-14 and color photo 2) is a whimsical work inspired by the lichen and tree fungus which grow near my home. A tiny inchworm wrapped with bright yellow embroidery floss climbs part of the work and others nest in the lidded basket nearby. The work is an example of the assemblage method many fiber artists use. Pieces are created separately and arranged to form the best design before being secured in place. An examination of each section of the disassembled work (fig. 5-15) should give you enough information to create

Fig. 5-14 "Lichen Bed." 12 x 10 x 4 inches.

Fig. 5-15 "Lichen Bed" disassembled.

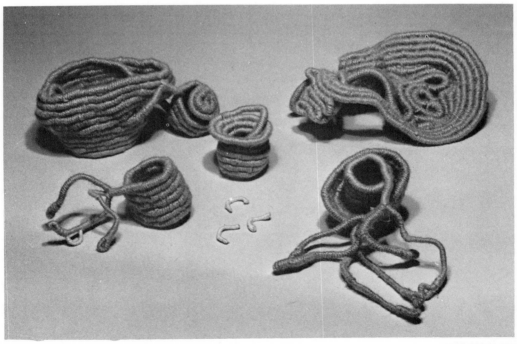

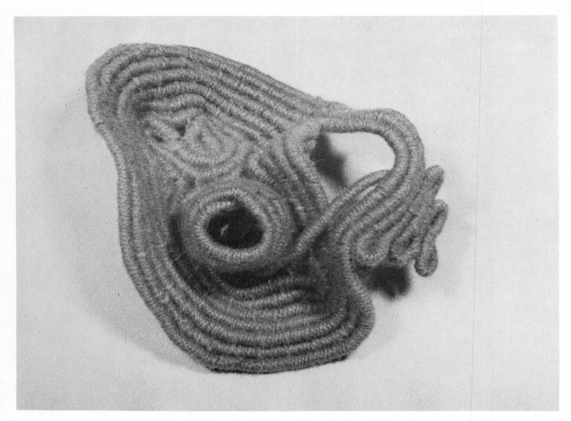

Fig. 5-16   The free-form mat base.

Fig. 5-17   The coiled design for the mat base, shown with a few of the attachments made.

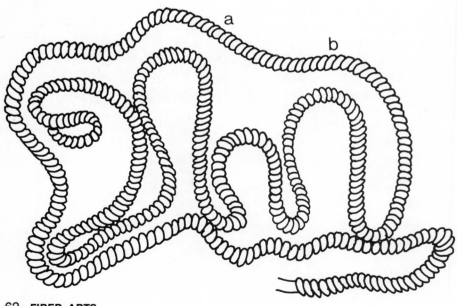

similar works based on free-form coiling and basketry techniques.

The warp for "Lichen Bed" is a three-ply jute, wrapped with grey-green and apple green wool.

The Free-Form Mat Base

The base of the sculpture is a cradlelike piece with an attached basket shape (fig. 5-16). It is begun as a free-form coiled mat. The maze of curving coils is begun with a 14-foot warp cord and follows the design illustrated in fig. 5-17. The grey-green wool-wrapped coils are attached with the figure-8 stitch at various points during construction of the piece, pulling some of the coils together and leaving others to project in open loops. When the basic form is completed, continue coiling around it, following it's abstract shape, and stitching the coils every few wraps to give the work a firm support. The first two coils that go around the abstract shape are placed on top of each other; after this, they are attached beside each other except in the small area between (a) and (b) in fig. 5-17. In this section, which will be behind the basket, the coils continue to climb on top of each other for two more rows, imparting a protruding shape to this part of the work.

The Detached Coils

The next two coils on the mat follow the previous ones, but they detach from the body of the work at a point indicated by (a) in fig. 5-17 and reattach near (b). A final coil follows the previous two, ending at (b) to bend back upon itself, as illustrated in fig. 5-18. The warp cord, which extends freely from the last bend, is wrapped with the same wool for 7 inches. It is then drawn underneath the detached coils, through the space, and over the body of the work to be stitched to the base mat in a position to begin the first basket shape. This position is best seen in fig. 5-16.

The Attached Basket

A basket with a 1½-inch-diameter round base is formed on the mat by coiling on top of the base mat coil for five rows. Two additional rows are added slightly inside the previous ones to bring the lip of the basket inward and partially close it. The basket

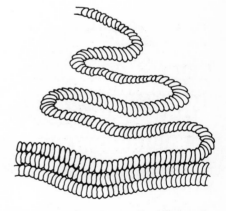

Fig. 5-18   The last coil of the mat bent back upon itself.

Fig. 5-19 Basket two with attached basket three.

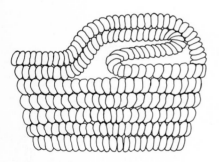

Fig. 5-20 The looped coil in basket two.

is completed by wrapping the jute warp for about 2 inches, fastening the weft end under the last few wraps, cutting the jute close to the wrapped end, and tucking it inside the basket.

Baskets Two and Three

A 5-yard warp cord is used to create the double basket section of "Lichen Bed," shown in fig. 5-19. The large (4-inch-diameter) basket is begun with an oval-shaped base. Apple green wool coils connect beside each other for four rows; then they wind on top of each other to climb for another two rows. Two rows of grey-green wool continue the basket, but these are joined slightly outside of the previous rows, causing the basket shape to enlarge and move outward. The next row consists of the detached loop coiling illustrated in fig. 5-20. This type of work changes the regular oblong shape of the basket into a more free-form coiled structure. The spaces created by the looping will receive the snakelike wrapped warp extensions which lead to and from the smaller basket. Five more rows of grey-green coiling continue the outward-directed shaping of the basket, following the outline of the looped coiling.

When the last row of coiling is completed on basket two, wrap the warp cord for about 4 inches and bring it inside the basket to exit through one of the openings formed by the loops. This wrapped cord is now turned over itself, as shown in fig. 5-21, to begin the base of basket three. This small basket has a 1½-inch diameter at the top and is made of six rows of coiling. When this basket is completed, the warp cord is again wrapped for about 7 inches and re-enters the large basket via another of the loop-formed openings. There the coil is ended by doubling it back upon itself to be wrapped and fastened.

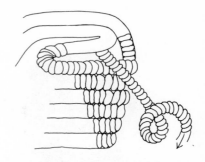

Fig. 5-21 Beginning attached basket three.

The small basket lid is formed by taking a 7-inch piece of warp and wrapping it with grey-green wool to form two coils and a 2-inch extension of the warp cord. The wrapped warp extension is stitched to the inside of the small basket, thereby securing the lid, which may be closed or left open to expose the inchworms sitting inside.

Inchworms

The four inchworms (but add as many as you like) are formed by wrapping a single ply of jute with yellow embroidery floss. Allow the warp end to extend a bit beyond the wrapping to prevent the weft from unraveling.

Small Baskets

Use a warp cord about 4 feet long to create each of the small baskets shown in figs. 5-22, 5-23, and 5-24. Try the line stitch or lace stitch on some of these baskets, if you like.

Basket four (fig. 5-22) is wrapped with apple green weft and has a round base of about a 1½-inch diameter. It consists of ten rows of coiling, with the last three rows directed outward to form the lip design. A 5-inch wrapped warp extension is tucked inside the basket to form another loop.

Basket five (fig. 5-23) begins with an oval base and is composed of nine rows of coiling, wrapped with grey-green wool. Three coils make the base. Each of the six rows of coiling which bring the basket sides up are attached slightly inside the previous rows, causing the coiling to narrow a bit as it climbs. After the last coil is attached, the warp is wrapped in the same wool for about 1 inch; then it is unplied, and each ply is wrapped with grey-green and apple green yarns. The warp extensions, which are finished by looping and wrapping, twist

Fig. 5-22   Basket four.

Fig. 5-23   Basket five.

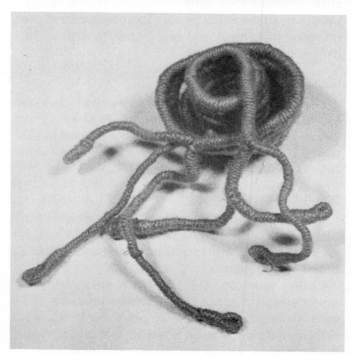

Fig. 5-24   Baskets six and seven.

and kink naturally as they are wrapped and require no wire core as they are small enough to support their own weight. The yellow inchworm which crawls along one of the extensions is added during the wrapping process.

Basket six, which sits inside basket seven (fig. 5-24), is composed of nine rows of coiling using an apple green weft yarn. The base is a 1-inch-diameter circle, and the coiling climbs straight up to end in a wrapped warp extension which is unplied to branch and then unplied to branch again, as shown. The plies are cut to unequal lengths.

Basket seven is wrapped with grey-green weft and has a 1½-inch-diameter oval base. Its walls are seven rows of outward-shaped coils, and it ends with three uneven wrapped extensions of unplied warp.

Assembling

Manipulate the separate baskets comprising "Lichen Bed" to see the variety of clusters possible before selecting and assembling a final arrangement. Assemble the parts, using the figure-8 stitch, either in the form shown in fig. 5-14 or in a form reflecting your own sense of design.

CROCHET

During the past few years, crochet has leaped from the antimacassared arms of overstuffed furniture and the blanketed legs of convalescents to the contemporary fiber art scene. It's somewhat ironic that the former pastime of refined gentlefolk should have become the most versatile and imaginatively used of all the fiber media. The intricate patterns of off-white doilies are being transformed into outrageous free-form sculptures in an explosion of colors. Combined with other fiber techniques or employed alone, the ease with which small pieces of work are created and then assembled makes crochet a delightful and portable means of fiber construction.

TOOLS AND WORKING METHODS
Choosing Yarn and Hooks

You could crochet without tools, using only your fingers and a pair of scissors, but chances are that you'll be using a hook sooner or later, so it's wise to have a few on hand. Thin crochet hooks are used with thin yarns; larger ones are usually used with thicker yarns. I say "usually" because some fiber artists enjoy the loose stitches created when working a thin yarn with a very large crochet hook. You will probably never need the tiny steel hooks used only with very delicate threads. More than likely you will be using aluminum hooks ranging in size from C, the smallest, to K, the largest. In addition to hooks, have some weaving needles on hand, as they are useful for pulling loose ends into the finished work.

Use whatever yarns you like, matching them with an appropriate hook size. There's no need to cut or measure yarn since, in crochet, you work directly from a ball of yarn.

Holding the Hook and Yarn

Position some thin rug yarn on your left hand (if you're right-handed), as illustrated in fig. 6-2. The

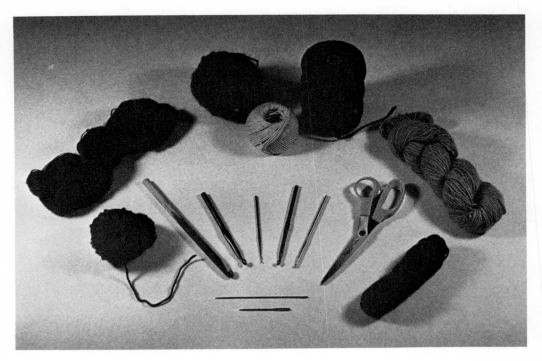

Fig. 6-1   Crochet supplies.

Fig. 6-2   One way to hold your crochet yarn.

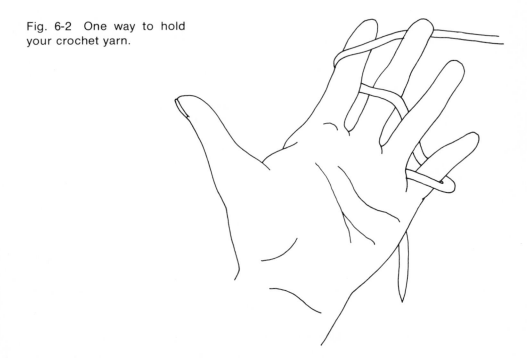

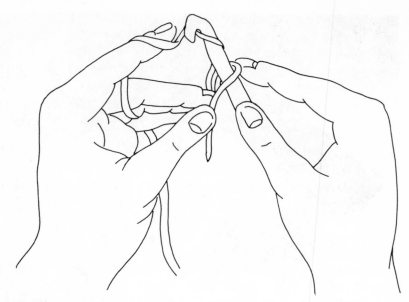

Fig. 6-3 An alternate method of holding your yarn, showing correct hook position.

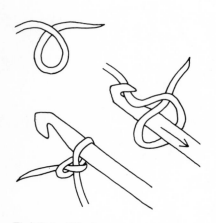

Fig. 6-4 Slip knot.

yarn goes over your ring finger, under your middle finger, and over your index finger, with the end wrapped around your little finger. In your other hand, hold a size F crochet hook, grasping the flat part of the hook between your index finger and thumb. Figure 6-3 shows the correct way to hold the hook and illustrates a different way to hold the yarn, with the end around the hook. Although the working position seems quite awkward at first, it will soon feel comfortable.

The Slip Knot

Begin crochet by attaching your yarn to the hook with a slip knot, formed about 4 inches from the cut end of the yarn. Create a loop as shown in fig. 6-4, and pass your hook through it. Then catch the long end of the yarn with the hook and pull through. Tighten your yarn strands to form a small loop around the hook, and you're ready to begin the row of chain stitches which is the foundation of all crochet pieces.

The Chain Stitch

Each piece of crochet is started from a row of chain stitches formed by catching the long yarn strand with your hook (also called "yarning over") and pulling this strand through the loop on the shank of your crochet hook (fig. 6-5). Continue yarning over and pulling through each single loop to form the chain. Practice this until you can control the yarn tension enough to form evenly sized stitches on which to base your crochet work.

Basic Crochet Stitches

Single Crochet. Single crochet is a flat stitch which forms closely set rows of work (fig. 6-6). Begin this stitch, as illustrated in fig. 6-7, by inserting your hook into the second stitch of your foundation chain (a), picking up the top two loops of the chain stitch (b). Now catch the yarn with the hook, as shown in (b), and pull the yarn back through. This gives you two loops on your crochet hook (c). Yarn over your hook (d) and pull it through the two loops to leave a single loop on the hook (e). The first single crochet stitch is complete. Insert your hook into the next stitch and continue to form your first row of single crochet stitches. At the end of your first row, make one chain stitch and turn your work so that the reverse side is facing you before continuing.

Variations of Single Crochet. Three variations of single crochet, the ridge stitch, the Albanian stitch, and the cross stitch, are easily made. To create the ridge stitch, pick up only the back loop of each stitch in the former row of crochet. Pick up only the front loop to create the Albanian stitch. The cross stitch will result if you do single crochet yarning over from front to back instead of in the usual direction shown in fig. 6-7(d).

Double Crochet. Double crochet forms a taller stitch than single crochet, with openings between the barlike stitches (fig. 6-8). To create a double crochet stitch, follow the steps illustrated in fig. 6-9.

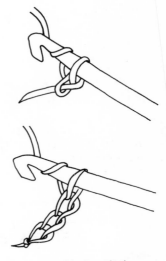

Fig. 6-5   Chain stitch.

Fig. 6-6   Three rows of single crochet.

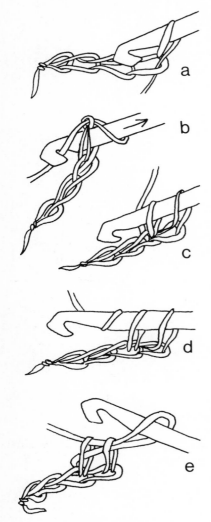

Fig. 6-7 Making one single crochet stitch.

Fig. 6-8 Three rows of double crochet.

First yarn over the hook and then enter the fourth stitch of your chain foundation, picking up the top two loops of the chain stitch (a). Catch the yarn on the hook, pull the yarn back through the stitch, and pull up a loop with the yarn. This gives you three loops on your hook (b). Yarn over again, (c) and pull the yarn through two loops (d). With two loops remaining on your hook, yarn over a third time and pull this yarn through the two remaining loops, creating the first stitch of double crochet (e). Make a double crochet in each stitch of the previous row before chaining three stitches and turning the work.

Treble Crochet. Treble crochet is a very tall stitch (fig. 6-10). It is begun, as shown in fig. 6-11, by yarning over your hook twice and entering the fifth stitch of the chain, picking up the top two loops of the chain stitch (a). Catch the yarn on the hook, pull it back through the stitch, and draw up a loop. This gives you four loops on your hook (b). Yarn over and pull your yarn through two of the loops. This leaves you with three loops on the hook (c). At this point, yarn over and pull the yarn through two loops; this leaves two loops (d). Yarn over again and pull through two loops. This gives you one loop on the hook and one complete stitch of treble crochet (e). Treble crochet in each remaining stitch in the previous row. At the end, chain four before turning to create a second row of crochet.

Decorative Stitches

Two decorative stitches, which are also useful for edging a piece of crochet, are the picot and the scallop. To make a picot, simply chain three and reenter the same stitch in which you began the chain. Then yarn over and draw the new loop

through the stitch and the loop on your hook. The bumplike projection is the picot. One or two single crochets may be worked between the picots.

The scallop is formed by chaining three, making a double crochet in the same space, and then skipping two stitches.

Increasing and Decreasing

The interesting shapes and ruffled edges of contemporary crochet are made using two simple techniques—increasing and decreasing. Increasing makes a work wider by adding more stitches in each row; decreasing makes it narrower by omitting stitches. To increase, simply do more than one stitch in a single space. One extra stitch can be made in each row of crochet to gradually build up a wider work, or one or more stitches can be made in each space to create a curling ruffle.

Decrease by combining two single stitches to make one. For example, to decrease in single crochet, begin a single crochet stitch, yarning over and pulling through, but as soon as you have two loops on your hook enter the next stitch. When you have three loops on your hook, yarn over and pull through all three loops. The same principle is applied when decreasing in other stitches.

Ending a Piece of Crochet

To end your crochet work, cut your yarn a few inches from the loop on your hook, yarn over, and pull the cut end through. The loose end should be

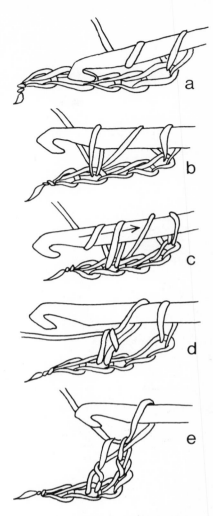

Fig. 6-9   Making one double crochet stitch.

Fig. 6-10   Three rows of treble crochet.

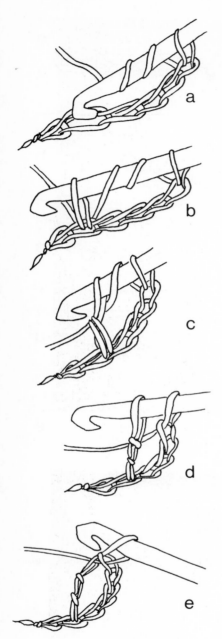

Fig. 6-11 Making one treble crochet stitch.

tightened and hidden by pulling it back into the work.

Adding on Yarn

When your ball of yarn is consumed or when you decide to switch to a different color in a work, you will need to join on a new piece of yarn. The most basic method of joining yarn is to tie on—knot the old yarn to the new and continue your crochet stitch. After the work is finished, you can untie the knot and weave the loose ends back into your work. Another method of joining involves treating both the old and new threads as one, making a stitch using both threads before dropping the old and continuing with the new one.

DISCOVERY: "FLOWER"

"Flower" (fig. 6-12) and the other crochet works in this chapter are the result of the joint efforts of sculptor Judith Wrend and myself. (The appeal of fiber sculpture may lure yet another metal sculptor from the acetylene tanks.) Ruth Gowell's incredible coiled and woven flower baskets (see color photos 10 and 15) impressed us both and moved us to do an interpretation of a flower in crochet. Although each piece of the work is two-dimensional, except for the projecting ruffled edges (fig. 6-13), assembling the pieces to create the flower gives it a sculptural form.

A size G crochet hook was used with medium weight green, white, and yellow wool yarns throughout the work. Yellow cotton floss is used for the stamen.

The First Ruffled Flower Center

The three flower centers are just crocheted circles. The smallest one is of green wool and uses the single crochet stitch. The single crochet is gradually increased to form a circle, and then drastically increased to form the ruffled edges. Make this first ruffled flower center as follows:

Begin the circle by doing five chain stitches and inserting your hook in the first chain stitch made, as illustrated in fig. 6-14. Then close the ring with a slip stitch by yarning over and pulling the yarn through both the chain stitch and the loop on your hook.

Fig. 6-12   "Flower." 3 inches high, 14-inch diameter.

Fig. 6-13   "Flower." disassembled.

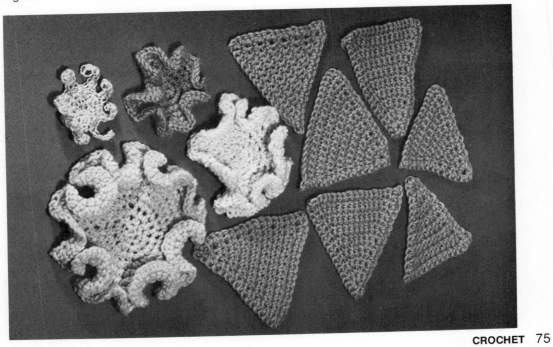

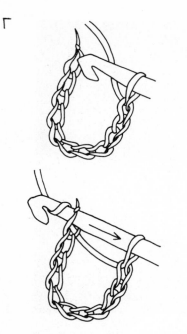

Fig. 6-14 Closing a chain stitch ring.

Continue forming your circle by working off the closed ring. For row one, chain two and do seven single crochet stitches. Close this round by inserting your hook into the first stitch of this row, yarning over and pulling through both loops. Then chain two and create the second row by making two single crochets in each stitch. Close this round as you did the first and create row three by chaining two and continuing around the circle, making one increase in every other stitch. Close this round and go on to row four by chaining two and making one single crochet in each stitch around the circle.

To form the ruffle, add two more rows of crochet to your circle, chaining two before making each round, and increase once in each stitch. Finish with a slip stitch, as described above under Ending a Piece of Crochet. The circle alone and the circle with ruffle are shown in fig. 6-15.

The Second Ruffled Flower Center

Using white wool, follow the directions for making the circle for the first ruffled flower center. Then add four more rows of crochet, chaining two before each round, and increasing in every stitch.

The Third Ruffled Flower Center

The third largest flower center begins with a larger, flat circle of yellow wool. Follow the direc-

Fig. 6-15 The circle before and after adding the ruffle.

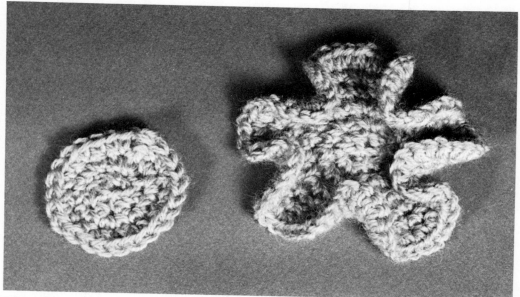

Fig. 6-16   The triangle before and after edging.

tions for making the small circle, but make six rows in all. In the fifth row, increase in every other stitch and in the sixth row, increase in every third stitch. To ruffle, add three more rows of single crochet, increasing in every stitch.

The Petals

The green wool petals of the flower are created by crocheting a triangle. Begin the tip of the triangle by chaining two and making one single crochet in the second chain stitch. Chain one and turn your work. Do three single crochets in your first single crochet stitch, chain one, and turn your work. Then do one single, make one increase in the second stitch, and continue across the row. Continue making one increase in the second stitch of each row until nine rows are completed.

To prevent the edges of your triangular petal from curling, edge it in single crochet. Using the yarn extending from your triangle, do one single crochet in each stitch around the outside of the triangle. Do three single crochets in the top stitch at the end of the point and omit the base of the triangle, which will be hidden by the flower centers. The petals before and after edging are shown in fig. 6-16.

Make seven petals in all.

The Stamen

The tiny curling flower center which represents the stamen of the plant (shown on the upper left in fig. 6-13) is made of bright yellow polished cotton floss. It is begun by making a circle containing two rounds (make the circle as described for the first ruffled flower center). Then insert your hook in the first stitch, yarn over and pull through, chain six, and crochet back down the chain, doing one single crochet in each chain stitch, reconnecting with the circle by doing the last single crochet in the second stitch of the circle. Insert your hook into the third stitch of the circle, chain six and crochet down the chain again. Continue making chained projections around the circumference of the circle, before closing the round with a slip stitch.

Assembling

Fasten the ends of each piece of crochet and pull any excess yarn back into the work. Stack the flower centers on top of each other and stitch them together with needle and yarn. Fasten the stamen to the middle of the small green flower center. Then arrange the green petals to form a circle, with the points radiating out and base points touching. Stitch the ends of the base points to each other; and stitch the stacked flower centers in place on top of the petals.

RELIEF WORK: "RAINCLOUD"

"Raincloud," pictured in figs. 6-17 and 6-18, was inspired by the cloud designs painted by the Pueblo Indians. To create this work, you'll crochet six small flat ovals and one large oval, which, folded and stuffed, will represent the cloud head. Then you'll crochet eleven spirals to suggest a rain shower. We used white, navy, and cornflower blue wool in this piece.

The Small Ovals

The ovals are formed with a single crochet stitch, increasing at each end of the oval to form the curve.

Begin your first round by chaining ten. Single crochet across the top of the foundation chain, doing three single crochets in the last chain stitch.

Fig. 6-17 "Raincloud." 10 x 34 x 3 inches.

Fig. 6-18 "Raincloud" disassembled.

Then single crochet across the bottom of the chain, doing three single crochets in the last chain stitch of that row. (Now you have increased at each end of the chain.) Close with a slip stitch.

For the second round, chain one and crochet down the side of the oval, making one increase in the stitch directly before the increase of the previous round. Then do one single crochet in the next stitch, followed by three singles in the one stitch at the top of the curve. Follow this increase with one single crochet in the next stitch. Do two single crochets in the next stitch and then continue with single crochet down the side of the oval to follow the same increasing pattern around the curve at the other end. Close round two with a slip stitch.

For round three, repeat the instructions used to make round two.

For round four, first chain one and single crochet down the side of the oval. For the top seven stitches of the curve, follow this pattern: two single crochets in the first stitch, one single crochet in each of the next two stitches, two single crochets in the fourth stitch, one single in each of the next two stitches and two single crochets in the seventh stitch. Continue down the side of the oval, repeating the pattern of increases on the other end of the oval. Then close the round with a slip stitch.

Make six ovals in all. Three of the small ovals are created with white wool, two are made with navy blue wool, and cornflower blue is used to make the sixth.

The Large Oval Cloud Head

Using cornflower blue wool, begin round one by chaining ten and doing one row of double crochet. In the last chain stitch, increase by doing seven double crochets in that stitch. Then double crochet across the other side of the chain, doing seven doubles in the last chain stitch of that row. Now you have increased at each end of the chain. Close the round with a slip stitch.

For round two, chain three and double crochet down the side of the oval. In the top five stitches of the curve, follow this pattern: two doubles in the first two stitches, three doubles in the third stitch, and two doubles in the last two stitches. Continue down the side of the oval with double crochet and follow the same pattern at the other curved end. Then close round two with a slip stitch.

For the third and fourth rounds, repeat the directions for round two.

For round five, chain three and double crochet down the side of the oval. Increase by doing two double crochets in each of the nine top stitches at each curve. Close the round with a slip stitch.

For round six, chain three and double crochet around the entire oval. Close with a slip stitch.

For the seventh and final round, follow the directions for round five. Close the round with a slip stitch.

Stuffing to Form Half Ovals

Place a stuffing material such as fiber fill on one end of each oval and fold the oval in half, creating a half oval. Edge each stuffed form with single crochet to finish and close it.

The Rain Shower

The eleven corkscrew spirals are created by chaining for a distance and then working down the chain, doing two single crochet stitches in each chain stitch. Make your rain shower spirals as long as you like (our longest measured 24 inches), and leave a tail of yarn on them to facilitate assembling.

Assembling and Hanging

With yarn, stitch the stuffed and spiral forms to each other, as pictured in fig. 6-17, pulling all yarn ends to the inside of the work. Attaching a loop on the back of the work will facilitate hanging.

SCULPTURE: "FACTORY TOWN"

"Factory Town" (figs. 6-19 and 6-20 and color photo 16) began with one smoking volcanic form. It looked so lonely, we decided to create another. Soon we had a city of forms which looked a lot more like Bayonne, New Jersey, than Mt. Vesuvius. A few narrow smoke stacks and some multi-colored smoke curls completed the work: a whimsical look at a rather serious topic.

Because cone-shaped crochet work tends to spiral, a simple increase pattern is maintained throughout the work to help minimize twisting in the cones. The cones are begun at the top, narrow

Fig. 6-19 "Factory Town." 8 x 13 x 4¹/₂ inches.

Fig. 6-20 "Factory Town" disassembled.

end, and flared outward to completion. We used shades of green and beige wool for the cones and stacks, and a variety of colors for the smoke curls.

The Narrow Stack Cones

The narrow stack cones, done in light and dark green wools, are begun with a chain stitch ring; some rings are five chains long, some are six. Single crochet stitches are used throughout. At 1-inch intervals, do a row with an increase in every third stitch to slightly flare the cone. Continue working until you reach the desired height.

The Wide Stack Cones

Longer chained rings—of seven or eight stitches—will give you wider mouths for your stacks. Increasing in every third stitch at 1/2-inch intervals will give these cones greater flare.

The Smoke Curls

The smoke curls, of various colors and lengths, are begun by making a base chain and then crocheting along it, creating spirals by doing two single crochets in each chain stitch. Separate the ply of some of your yarns and use a small crochet hook to create wispier curls.

Assembling

Insert the ends of your smoke curls into your completed stacks and rearrange the pieces to see the various forms possible. Perhaps you'll find a grouping more pleasing than the one pictured. Then, using wool yarn, stitch the pieces together and pull all loose ends to the inside of the work. Although we enjoy the relaxed look of the unstuffed stacks you may want to stiffen your structures by filling them with fiber fill.

WEAVING

TOOLS AND WORKING METHODS

A complete list of tools and equipment for weaving could no doubt fill a good portion of this book. Floor looms, table looms, inkle, backstrap, weighted looms, etc., enable you to weave various sized pieces at various speeds. Beaters, swords, quills, and bobbins lead the long accessory list. The language of weaving is melodious and beautiful; the Scandinavian implements dazzling—and expensive. The most beautiful Oriental carpets and complicated contemporary weavings are, however, often the result of weaving on a simple frame loom.

To begin weaving you'll need an inexpensive loom, scissors, a fork or comb to beat down the weft yarns, and a weaving needle or bodkin to carry your weft yarns through the warp strands. Although not essential, a ruler or paint-stirring stick is helpful in forming a shed or passageway through the warp yarns so that your needle-carried weft can be woven more rapidly.

Fig. 7-1 Weaving supplies.

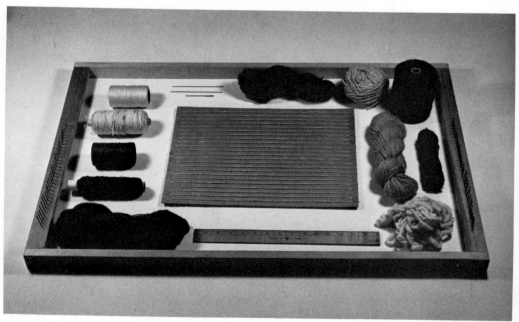

Constructing and Warping Simple Looms

Cardboard Loom. The cardboard loom can be constructed from a piece of masonite, heavy artboard, or from the cardboard box inserts discarded by grocery stores. For small works, the $12^1/_2'' \times 16^1/_4''$ box inserts are perfect. Using an X-acto knife or scissors, cut evenly spaced notches along the top and bottom of the cardboard to accept your warp cords (fig. 7-2). The weft or filler yarns are later woven up and down through the warp cords. Starting $1/_4$ inch in from the edge of the cardboard, notch the board at $1/_4$-inch intervals. The notches could be further apart, depending upon your requirements for each particular work. Begin warping by knotting or taping the end of the warp cord behind the upper first notch in your cardboard. Warp as illustrated in fig. 7-2, passing the warping cord down the front of the cardboard and into the first notch at the bottom of the loom, then under the small piece of cardboard and through the second bottom notch to the front of the loom again. Then carry the warp up to the second notch at the top of the loom. Continue warping the loom, maintaining a firm, even tension in the warp. Tape the warp end to the back of the loom after it passes through the last notch in the cardboard.

Wooden Frame Loom. Wooden frame looms can be constructed from a variety of materials. Picture frames, canvas stretchers, old window screen supports, even vegetable crates can be used. A simple yet sophisticated-looking loom, like the one shown in fig. 7-3, can be made for about two dollars. Evenly spaced nails may be added to the top and bottom ends of the frame loom to hold the warp, or the loom may be warped by winding cord around the frame without using nails. To warp with nails, tie the end of the warp to the first nail at one end of the loom and pass it down and around the corresponding nail at the bottom of the loom. Bring the cord back up and around the second nail at the top of the loom, etc. After warping is completed, the cord is knotted to the last nail.

The partially completed, shaped weaving pictured in fig. 7-4 is being woven by Anne Mitchell on a frame loom warped by simply winding the cord around the frame. Heavy masking tape can be used

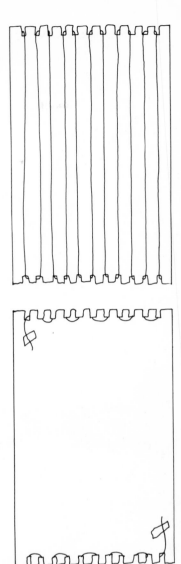

Fig. 7-2 Front and back of a warped cardboard loom.

Fig. 7-3 Constructing a wooden frame loom. The corner supports are glued in.

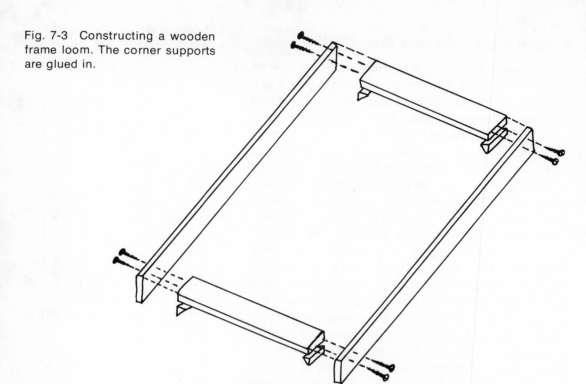

Fig. 7-4 Loom warped by winding around the frame. Weaving by Anne Mitchell.

1 "African shovel mask—Morani." Author. 14″ x
45″. A found object—a rusted shovel—inspired this
mask, composed of macrame and wrapping
techniques.

2 "Lichen Bed." Author. 12″ x 10″ x 4″. Several baskets are assembled to create this coiled work, based on the forms of lichen and tree fungus.

3 "Ceremonial Mat." Author. 5½″ diameter. An Ethiopian straw mat inspired this coiled and wrapped work.

4 "Steps." Author. 16″ x 30″ x 3″. Three weavings, each woven on a round loom, are assembled to create this work, loosely patterned on a clay brick walk.

5 Ruth Gowell's natural dyes recordbook. The subtle and brilliant hues which spill from the pages of this notebook attest to Ruth's dyepot expertise and the capacities of natural dyes to color yarns. (Photo courtesy of the artist)

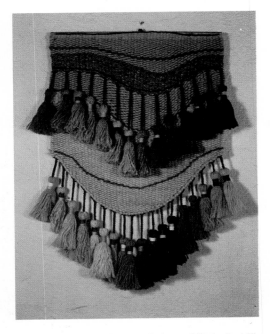

7 "Rainbow U.S.A." Ruth Geneslaw. 11″ x 25″ x 18″. The artist's discrete use of color and her concern with three-dimensional forms and the spaces which surround and inhabit them are apparent in this delightful landscape, a combination of weaving, crochet, and wrapping techniques. (Photo courtesy of the artist)

6 "Twelve and Twenty." Anne Mitchell. 14″ x 20″. Tapestry weaving. The braided warp with added tassels gives this work textural interest.

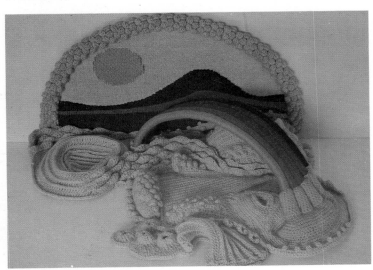

8 "The Five Seasons." Susan Aaron-Taylor. 6½′ x 8½′. Crochet and coiling techniques were used to depict the change in seasons through the change in flower and color groupings. The center mask shows the artist's interpretation of Michigan's weather. (Photo courtesy of the artist)

9 "Garuda." Anne Mitchell. 40″ x 60″. The combined images of a Chinese paper kite and a mythological Indian bird inspired this stuffed woven tapestry.

10 "Spring Flower." Ruth Gowell. 15″ diameter. Brazilwood and Queen Anne's Lace were used to dye the yarn for this coiled, woven, and chrocheted treasure basket. (Photo courtesy of the artist)

11 "Earthweave." Anne Mitchell. 32″ x 46″. The furrows of a newly ploughed field inspired this woven tapestry. The textures of various yarns and surface techniques suggest the textures in the soil.

12 "Shaman." Author. 12″ x 38″. A relief sculpture mask composed of clove hitches and supported by a metal armature. (Photo courtesy of the artist)

13 "Baroque Landscape." Ruth Geneslaw. 7″ x 28″. Weaving, crochet, spool knitting, and wrapping were used to create this fantasy work. The colors and corkscrew curls sustain the character of the piece. (Photo courtesy of the artist)

14 "Triangulation." Anne Mitchell. 14½″ x 8″. This weaving was mounted on a triangular wooden frame to repeat the miniature tapestry-woven triangles within it.

15 "Madder Bloom." Ruth Gowell. 9″ diameter. Madder root was used to dye the yarn for this flower-inspired sculpture. Weaving, coiling, and wrapping techniques were used. (Photo courtesy of the artist)

16 "Factory Town." Judith Wrend and author. 8″ x 13″ x 4½″. A whimsical interpretation of smoke stacks, created in crochet.

to hold the warp in place on the frame, if necessary.

Round Loom. Round looms can be employed to weave tubular works or, if you weave only part way around, to create rectangular or square pieces, as well. A cardboard salt box or wooden cable spool can be employed as looms (fig. 7-5), as well as other found objects, such as old lamp shades or large cardboard drums. Instructions for constructing a round loom are given later in this chapter along with directions for creating the tubular weaving "Steps."

Looms on Found Objects

Any object which will receive and hold the warp cords taut can be employed as a loom (fig. 7-6). You can wrap warp strands around a door to create a double-sided loom, around an old farming implement, branch, or even between the rungs of a stool. Attaching the warp cords to a branch or mounting bar with a lark's head knot and weighing down the loose warp ends with heavy objects represents still another method of setting up a makeshift loom.

Choosing a Warp

In selecting a warp, you must consider whether the material is strong enough to withstand the stress of receiving the weft cords and whether it's made of a fiber which will not stretch (stretching creates an uneven warp tension). You must also decide whether or not you want the warp cords to be visible in the finished weaving. A thick, nappy warp will show against a medium-weight filler; a narrow warp will not. In a weaving with exposed warp, different colored warp cords may be tied on to create a striped pattern.

Linen, cotton, and hemp are standard warping cords, but good quality jute and other fibers can also be used. Most of these warping fibers are available on small cones which allow you to pull the cord easily from the cone as you warp, eliminating the need for estimating warp length and making additional tie-ons.

Choosing a Weft

Just about any material can be used as a weft for weaving. As cords are pieced easily and often dur-

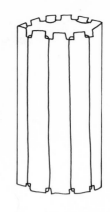
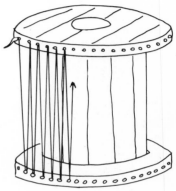

Fig. 7-5   Round looms. Salt box (top) and cable spool (bottom).

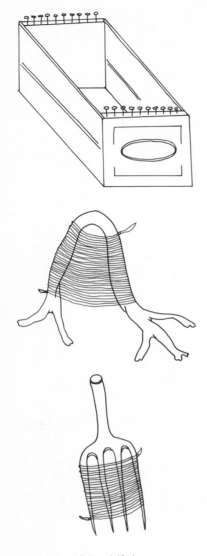

Fig. 7-6 Makeshift looms.

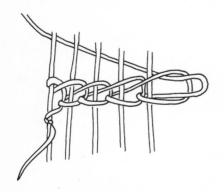

Fig. 7-7 Chained spacer.

ing weaving, the ply, elasticity, and strength of the weft is not crucial. In addition, unspun fibers, grasses and found objects can be easily manipulated through the warp threads with your fingers.

The Chained or Twined Spacer

The most difficult task for the new weaver is learning to keep the warp ends evenly spaced and avoiding the scalloped selvedge edges which occur when warp ends are pulled in by your weft. Using either the chained or twined spacing techniques illustrated in figs. 7-7 and 7-8 will help you space the warp ends initially.

The yarn used to make your row of chaining should be about five times the width of your loom and may be tied to the edge of the loom or to the last warp cord. Make a small loop of the chaining yarn and, with the looped end facing away from the edge of the loom, hold the loop over the first warp cord. With your fingers or a crochet hook, draw the chaining yarn underneath the first warp and through the loop. This makes another small loop (don't pull the chaining yarn all the way through). Hold this second loop over the second warp and pull through a third loop of the chaining yarn. Hold it over the third warp, and so on. Continue across the warp (fig. 7-7). If the chain is loose, it won't serve its purpose, so pull the loops tight enough to create a slight tension in the chain and to secure the warp cords the proper distance apart. Chaining may be done spanning single warps, or may cover two warps with each loop.

Twining is accomplished as shown in fig. 7-8 and may be used as a spacing device or as a technique for weaving an entire piece.

Forming the Shed

Creating a shed or opening between two layers of warp cords through which a weft yarn can be pulled speeds up the weaving process. On large floor looms and some frame looms two sheds are usually created. In the first shed, the even-numbered warp cords are lifted, forming a passageway for wefts carried from left to right, and in the second, the odd cords are lifted to receive cords carried in the opposite direction. Much needle and tapestry weaving, however, is done without any shed formations and relies on the needle, bobbin, or fingers to carry the weft above and below the warp ends.

If you want to create a shed in your weaving, simply weave a ruler or stick up and down among the warp cords and flip the stick on edge to form the shed (fig. 7-9). Flatten it again for the next row of weaving. With this kind of simple arrangement you can make a shed only for every other row of your weaving.

Tabby or Plain Weave

The simple, sturdy, over-under, over-under pattern of the tabby or plain weave is familiar to almost everyone. Variations in warp and weft, texture and color, and warp manipulation can give you numerous design possibilities using only this basic weave. You can begin weaving at the edge of your warp, leaving a few inches of weft yarn extending in a tail which can later be woven into the back of the finished work. Or you may begin weaving in the center of the warp cords, as seen in fig. 7-10, and work toward the outside of the loom, using the same technique employed for piecing the yarn (see below).

Fig. 7-8   Twined spacer.

Fig. 7-9   Forming a shed with a ruler.

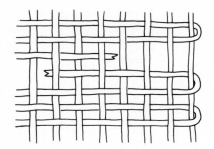

Fig. 7-10   The tabby weave and piecing the yarn.

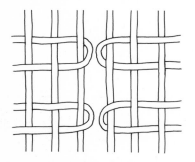

Fig. 7-11   Straight slit.

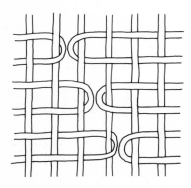

Fig. 7-12   Diagonal slit.

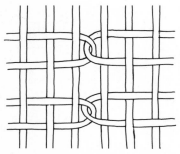

Fig. 7-13   Straight interlock.

Beating

Beating is pushing the weft yarns into place against the last row of weaving. It can be done with a tapestry comb or beater, a fork, a weaving needle, or with your fingers. Whatever you use, take care that you use the same force behind each beat. Your moods and feeling will show in your weaving, and the weavings of people with uneven tempers sometimes have a distinctly uneven look about them. Weft yarns should be laid in at an angle, rather than straight across, before being beaten down, as this will allow you to ease the weft against the warp, preventing the draw-in problem of a weft too tightly pulled.

Adding New Weft

Weft cords longer than 3 yards become difficult to handle without tangling, and trying to pass a lump of yarn through your warp strands is definitely counterproductive. Weave with a comfortably short weft cord; piecing the yarn, as illustrated in fig. 7-10, becomes second nature once you've done it a few times.

Basic Tapestry Techniques

Tapestry weaving is an ideal technique to use for creating works with abstract or representational designs. In tapestry, all warp cords are covered with the plain weave, but instead of carrying a continuous weft from one edge of the work to the other, the weaver covers the warp in sections. Colors are introduced and shapes built as blocks of warp are filled with different wefts.

There are several ways to join color areas in tapestry weaving. The slit technique, illustrated in figs. 7-11 and 7-12, functions as a design element or to join different color areas. As the yarns on either side of the slit do not share a warp cord, an open slit is formed between the two areas. Bundled weft cords may be woven through these openings or narrow woven strips can be passed through them, as well.

The interlock technique, shown in figs. 7-13 and 7-14, is another way to smoothly join blocks of two different colored wefts. The interlock can also be used at the end of each row by looping one weft through the other; this is useful when you have very frequent color changes, as in a horizontal stripe pattern, for instance.

In the dovetail technique, the different colored weft cords encircle a common warp (figs. 7-15 and 7-16). The jagged effect produced with this method of joining is more pronounced if several rows are finished on one side before coming back with the different colored weft on the other side.

Surface Texture Techniques

The texture of your weaving will be greatly affected by the type of weft you use—whether it is nubby or smoothly spun wool, a smooth and sturdy linen, wild grasses, ribbon, etc. But there are other ways to add special textural effects. Three ways to give dimension to an otherwise flat weaving— ghiordes knots, soumak stitch, and looping—are described below. The ghiordes or oriental knot is created by laying a piece of cut weft over two warps and pulling the ends of the weft around and up between the warp ends, as shown in fig. 7-17. Pull the warp ends toward you and against the previous row of weaving to position them. A row of plain weave should be placed after each row of ghiordes knots to facilitate beating and to hold them in place.

An alternate way of forming the ghiordes knot is to use a dowel or pencil, as illustrated in fig. 7-18. Working from left to right, the weft passes over the dowel (as on the far left in fig. 7-18), spans two warps, goes under the dowel and back underneath one of the warps, then around and over two warps, back underneath one, and over the dowel again. The knots may be tightened and cut against the dowel with a razor blade or the rod may be removed and the knots beaten into place to form uncut loops.

Another method of creating surface texture consists of weaving a loose row of tabby and using a crochet hook or your fingers to pull up loops of weft (fig. 7-19). As in making the ghiordes knot, a row of weaving should follow each row of looping to hold the work in place.

The soumak stitch is another way to create a surface pattern on your weaving. The soumak weft is carried over two warp cords and back under one, as illustrated in fig. 7-20. As with all surface texture

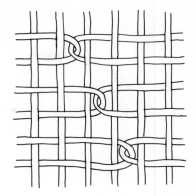
Fig. 7-14   Diagonal interlock.

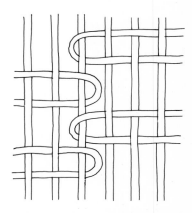
Fig. 7-15   Straight dovetail.

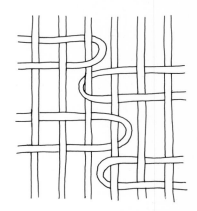
Fig. 7-16   Diagonal dovetail.

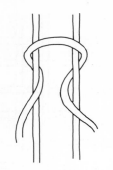

Fig. 7-17   Ghiordes knot.

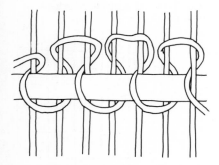

Fig. 7-18 Forming loops of ghiordes knots.

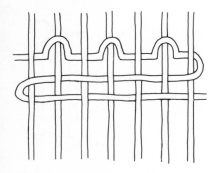

Fig. 7-19   Forming loops from a row of tabby weave.

techniques, care must be taken to beat each row firmly without distorting the warp. Variations of soumak are possible by spanning more warps with each stitch or by reversing the direction of the soumak and working it diagonally as well.

Finishing and Mounting

Weavings can be finished in a variety of ways. Warp ends may be wrapped, braided, or may extend freely at each end of your weaving. A row or two of macrame may be added to the base of a work, but be sure it doesn't become overly decorative and distract from the weaving. Any extending warp or weft ends may be woven back into the piece to create an unfringed weaving (fig. 7-21) or a hem may be turned under and stitched at either end.

The finishing touches can enhance or totally ruin a work, so be sure to consider the design and character of your weaving when choosing a mounting bar. Some weavings look terrific tacked to the underside of a piece of barnwood; others would be destroyed if they were hung by anything but a hidden loop. You can pass a mounting bar through knotted warp cords or turn a fringed edge under and stitch to form a passageway for an invisible mounting bar. There was a time when it was considered unethical to use a technique other than weaving to finish a woven piece, but the feeling today is that one should use any methods necessary to achieve a desired effect. Some weavers even sew their woven edges around a metal framework (a found object, for example, or an armature, as in fig. 8-18) to create a relief form from their weaving.

DISCOVERY: "EARTH STRATA"

Loosely patterned on the images of a tree, root formations and rock layers, "Earth Strata" (fig. 7-22) can be woven on a frame or cardboard loom that is at least 12 inches wide and 20 inches long. The warp used in this weaving is narrow, off-white cotton warp cord. The warp strands were spaced 1/8 inch apart across a 10-inch weaving width to form a compactly woven piece, but you could use fewer warp strands and space them further apart, modifying the directions, if you choose. The weft is off-white, apple green, dark green, bronze, and yellow wool.

Like many woven pieces, this one is worked upside down, that is, the design is woven from top to bottom. At first you will want to turn the loom often during the weaving process, as the idea of working in this position seems a little distressing. Soon you will grow accustomed to a new way of visualizing your weaving.

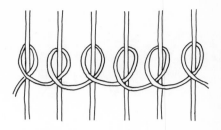

Fig. 7-20 Soumak.

The Heading

Begin the heading by tabby weaving a 3/4-inch-tall section with off-white wool. (Draw-in is not a particular problem in this piece, so no warp spacer is required.) End your white weft and piece in a strand of apple green wool; weave with the green yarn for 1/2 inch. Then do three rows of looping with bronze wool, remembering to tabby weave between each one. One half inch of tabby-woven bronze wool completes the heading.

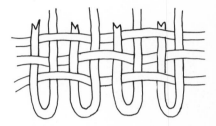

Fig. 7-21 Weaving warp ends in.

Left and Right Woven Sections

An exaggerated slit technique is employed now. The warp is divided into three sections to be woven separately for over 8 inches. The left and right sections each contain approximately one-fourth of the warp strands. Tabby weave these warp strands for 1 1/2 inches with white wool. Then split each of these sections using the tapestry slit technique and weaving for another 1 1/2 inches before rejoining the warp and closing the slit. These narrow slits can be seen in the white sections just under the heading on either side of the weaving in fig. 7-23. Tabby weave with the white wool for another 1/2 inch, and then make two rows of ghiordes knots with the same wool.

Apple green wool is now woven for 1/2 inch. Then the warp is split again, with slightly more of the warp on the outside portion of the division. The apple green wool is continued for 2 3/4 inches down the portion of warp closest to the center of the work. White plain weave follows the green for 1 1/2 inches. The outside, larger section of warp is now woven with 1/2 inch of yellow wool, followed by 3 inches of bronze, two rows of yellow ghiordes knots, and another 2 inches of bronze plain weave.

Central Woven Section

Dovetail Tree Design. Begin the abstract tree design shown in the top center of the weaving by weaving a few rows of tabby with the bronze wool. Then begin tapering the weaving to a center point by omitting the two outside warp strands on each row until your final three rows of tabby cover only the three center warp ends. Do not cut the bronze yarn—just lay it aside for the moment. Using the yellow wool, fill in two large points, following the bronze diagonal line, weaving until you've formed a horizontal line even with the last row of bronze wool (see fig. 7-23). These yellow points can be created by using the dovetail technique or by outlining the points with a row of tabby and then filling in. (A design of your own could be used in this area, as well.) You'll probably notice your warp drawing in a bit in these divided sections—don't worry

Fig. 7-22 "Earth Strata." 9¹/₂ x 18 inches.

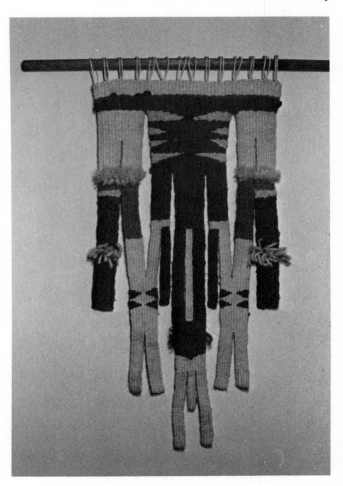

Fig. 7-23   Detail of "Earth Strata."

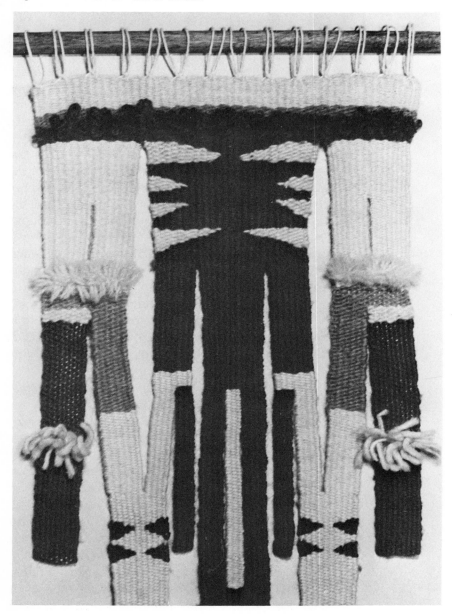

about this as the slight draw-in is used as part of the design. The yellows wefts need not be cut and ended because they can be carried across the back of the work or carried along the edges of the outermost warps and woven over when the bronze wool is employed again.

Six more large points of bronze are created, three extending from each side of a solid bronze center, and four small yellow points are filled in as the weaving progresses. The final triangles of yellow tabby weave begin at the horizontal base of the bronze tree motif and end on a slight diagonal, complementing the top diagonal lines of the first yellow points. The yellow wefts should be dropped in back of the warp now as they will not be used again. The bronze yarn is used again to fill in below the yellow points and then to cover all the warp cords in the section with several rows of tabby weave.

Central Strip. The warp is now divided into three sections, the center strip containing slightly more warps than the side areas. Tabby weave the center strip for 3 inches using the bronze wool. Then divide the center strip into three narrow sections. Two bronze 4½-inch-long bands flank a 4½-inch-long white band (see fig. 7-23), and then all warp strands in the center strip are again joined with the bronze wool. Continue to tabby weave for 1 inch, add two rows of ghiordes knots, and end with another inch of tabby, tapering the bronze color to a point in the center of the warp (see fig. 7-22). End the bronze weft and complete the center strip with three separate bands of white.

Adjacent Strips and Connecting the Woven Sections. Begin the two other strips of the central woven section by tabby weaving with the bronze wool for 2¾ inches, weaving a ½ inch section of white, and then dividing each strip into two narrow bands. The bands closest to the center of the work are filled with bronze wool for 3½ inches, which completes them.

The outside bands receive 2¾ inches of white wool; this should make them even with the white weaving done in the left and right woven sections. The 8-inch slit is closed as the warp cords in these two sections are filled with ½ inch of white wool (see fig. 7-23). A white diamond shape is created and small green points filled in before the white wool continues over all warp ends for 1 inch. Then the warps are separated into two equal sections and tabby woven with white for 2$^1/_2$ inches.

Removing the Weaving from the Loom

To remove "Earth Strata" from the loom, cut the warp about 2 inches from the ends of the woven strips and slip the other warp ends that connect the heading to the loom off the nails or cardboard.

Finishing and Mounting

Knot the warp loops at the top of your weaving in groups of two or three and needle weave any un-looped warp ends into the back of the work. The edges of the strips at the bottom of the weaving should be turned under about $^1/_8$ inch and all ex-tending warp ends should be woven into the back of the work, passing through several rows of weaving before being trimmed. Strands of pieced weft should be needle woven back in and clipped at this time as well.

The narrow strips will curl naturally when they are removed from the loom. This can be remedied by covering them with a slightly damp cloth and lightly pressing with an iron, being careful not to flatten any ghiordes knots.

Use a sanded and stained wooden dowel to hang the work, or else choose another mounting device, bearing in mind that the colors, slit weaving, and surface techniques have given the work quite a bit of detail which calls for a simple mounting.

RELIEF WORK: "RECTANGULAR 8S"

This small hanging (fig. 7-24) is loosely patterned on the oriental ownership stamps used to mark Japanese watercolors and drawings. Woven on an 10$^1/_2''$ × 16$^1/_2''$ cardboard loom, it has four finished selvedges and can be hung either horizontally or vertically. When hung vertically, the slits open slightly to form projections in the work. The weaving could be done on either a frame or a cardboard loom and made smaller or larger as desired. "Rectangular 8s" was woven in a horizontal position, with the loom warped with thin hemp cord at $^1/_4$ inch intervals across a 12-inch weaving width. Rust

Fig. 7-24 "Rectangular 8s."
9½ × 12 inches.

wool, a grey and brown flecked homespun, and teal blue hemp were used in this work.

The Outer Border

Rust wool is used to create the outer rectangular border, which sets up the boundaries of the weaving and gives a 1½ inch wide border to the work. The border is needle woven in two L-shaped sections. First one L is woven, and then the loom is turned to create the second L.

To weave the L, make a 1½-inch-wide section of tabby along the bottom horizontal foot of the L-shape. The last row of weave should be directed toward the left to begin the left vertical side of the rectangle. Six warp strands are covered with tabby weave, forming a woven section 1½ inches wide. Weave until the vertical band is 1½ inches from the top edge of the warp cords. Cut the weft, leaving a short tail. Now turn the loom around and repeat the directions to form the second L (fig. 7-25). This completes the first rectangular shape.

The Center Band

The large rectangular border is divided by a center band into two smaller rectangles. This post

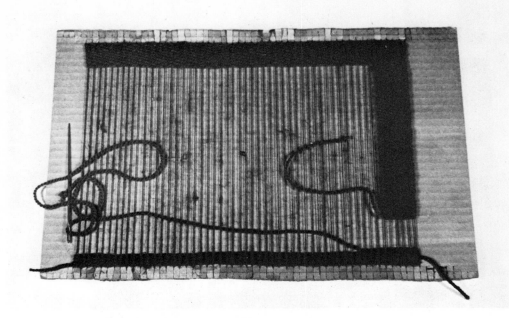

is woven in rust wool, using the tabby weave, over the five center most warp strands. When the band is completed, the weaving looks very much like two barred windows. The exposed warp strands could be wrapped at this time, giving a totally different feeling to the work.

Fig. 7-25 Beginning the second L-shaped section of the outer border.

The Inner Borders

The areas of warp on either side of the center band each receive another smaller rectangular border, woven in the same way as the large outer border, except that the vertical sides are woven over five, not six, warp strands and are thus a bit narrower. I've used a grey and brown flecked homespun wool for these rectangular borders. They contrast with the rust border in both color and texture and because an open slit separates them on their long sides. The interlocking weave could be employed to attach the two rectangular borders, if desired, but I enjoy the protrusions of the sections as they pull away from each other.

Wrapped Weft Bundles

Four $6^1/_2$-inch-long bundles of hemp strands are wrapped and used as decorative pieces of weft at the ends of the innermost rectangles. The bundles

Fig. 7-26 The weaving before completing the second inner rectangle.

contain ten strands of teal blue hemp warping cord and are wrapped for $2^1/_2$ inches in the center of the bundle with strands of hemp extending on either side of the wrapping. A fifth bundle of hemp, 13 inches long, is wrapped for 1 inch in the middle of the bundle and for $2^1/_2$ inches on either side beginning 2 inches in from the ends. This long weft will span both sections of the weaving and will project forward to give more depth to the work.

The Inner Rectangles

Using your fingers, tabby weave one of the small weft bundles through the remaining warp strands to begin each solid rectangle within the grey borders. Rust wool is woven and beaten down against these bundles to a point half way up the warp cords. The 12-inch bundle of weft is then finger woven into the next row (see fig. 7-26). Put the remaining two weft bundles at the tops of the rectangles. Then weave a few more rows with rust wool to complete the work.

Removing and Mounting the Work

Remove the weaving from the loom by slipping the warp loops off the loom. Trim the cardboard if

Fig. 7-27 "Steps." 16 x 23 x 3 inches.

necessary so you don't have to cut the warp loops. Several hemp strands are threaded through a large-eyed needle and then passed through the warp loops to create fiber mounting bars at the top and bottom of the work (see fig. 7-24). Dowels could be used, but I preferred not to add another color or texture to the piece. The non-looped strands of warp are caught in a 1-inch wrap at each end of the fiber mounting bars.

Hang the work horizontally for a while and then observe it in a vertical position for a different impression of the piece.

SCULPTURE: "STEPS"

"Steps" consists of three weavings assembled to hang as one (fig. 7-27 and color photo 4). The piece was inspired by a fascinating clay floor composed of loose bricks which made musical clicking sounds when walked upon. Because they are woven on a round loom, the cylinders have four selvedges and no seams. They are stuffed and stitched closed at the top and bottom to become plump pouches. I wove this piece with shades and textures of grey, brown, white, and rose wool. Either a cotton or linen warp cord works well.

Constructing a Round Loom

The round loom on which the weavings were created is illustrated in figs. 7-28 and 7-29. It consists of two 3³/₄-inch-diameter circles cut from a 1-inch-thick pine board, supported by two pieces of scrap wood, each 6 inches long. The loom is assembled as shown, using small nails to secure the top and bottom circles to the upright supports. Do not pound the nails holding the top circle onto the supports all the way in. Then the top of the loom may be lifted off for easy removal of the finished weaving. Using a tape measure and starting from the same spot on the top and bottom circles, make a pencil mark every ¹/₂ inch around the circumference of the circles. Hammer #6 upholsterer's tacks halfway in at these marked spots to make an easily removable warp support. The tacks remain firm enough to hold the warp securely but will pull out for removing the finished warp. You may want to remove some of these tacks in the future for a more widely spaced warp on another weaving.

Warping the Round Loom

Begin warping with a narrow cotton or linen warp cord, tying one end of the warp to a tack on the upper circle. Warp down, around, and up to the next nail and continue to warp the entire loom (fig. 7-29). When done warping, cut the warp strand and tie it to the last tack on the bottom circle of the loom.

The First Round Weaving

When the loom is warped, begin the weaving by first creating a chained spacer to evenly distribute the warp strands. The grey wool chained spacer continues around the circumference of the loom and leads directly into a ¹/₂-inch-high section of grey tabby weave. Another ¹/₂-inch-high section is

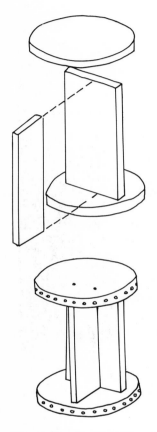

Fig. 7-28 Constructing the round loom.

Fig. 7-29 Warping the round loom.

Fig. 7-30 The first round weaving on the loom.

Fig. 7-31 The completed first round weaving.

woven, using a heavy handspun brown and grey flecked wool. Two rows of soumak follow, made with a rose colored wool. Then rows of red-brown heavy wool are tabby woven to fill a $3/4$-inch area. Next a heavy thick and thin handspun white wool continues for five rows of tabby weave, filling another $3/4$ inches of the weaving. The grey homespun is used to create a row of ghiordes knots, and these are followed by tabby weave with the same yarn, covering a $2^1/2$-inch area. A dark grey handspun wool is now tabby woven for $1/2$ inch, followed by a row of looping. On the round loom looping is accomplished by simply tabby weaving through several warp cords and then pulling loops of weft up with your fingers or a crochet hook. Loops irregular in size will add even more texture to the weaving. Two rows of tabby weave secure the first row of loops; then a second row of loops is created. Continue tabby weaving with the dark grey wool (fig. 7-30) to bring the weaving to just below the tacks at the top of the loom.

Removing the Work from the Loom

To remove your weaving from the round loom, pull out the tacks holding the warp cords and lift off the top of the loom. The weaving will slide over the post supports.

Stuffing and Adding the Wrapped Fringe

The bottom of the weaving (the edge closest to the dark grey looping) is closed by collapsing the form so that it is flat and passing a single strand of yarn through several (e.g., two or three) warp loops to draw the ends of the work together. Seven strands of heavy, thick-and-thin wool are used to join seven groups of loops in the work shown. The added strands are wrapped with grey wool for distances varying from 2 to 8 inches, and the single loose warp end is absorbed as part of the wrapped core. Note in fig. 7-31 that the lengths of the fringes vary.

A stuffing material, such as dryer lint, wool clippings, fiber fill, etc., is then used to loosely fill the woven form. Any warp loops that extend from the top of the weaving are then tucked inside, and grey wool is used to stitch the top closed.

The Tassels

Tassels of flecked homespun wool, wrapped with rust-brown wool, are added to the two outside wrapped fringes as follows. About twenty 4-inch-long wool pieces are cut and held against the wrapped fringe, as shown on the left in fig. 7-32. First they are wrapped to secure them to the strands of heavy wool, then the pieces are clipped close to the wrapping and pulled down, covering the area just wrapped. A final 1-inch wrap with the rust-brown wool, which bundles the flecked pieces together (see fig. 7-32, right), completes the tassels.

The Second and Third Round Weavings

Two more round weavings are created, using the same weaving sequence employed for the first part of "Steps." The forms are closed and stuffed in the same way, except that the wrapped fringes on the third, bottom part of the hanging are longer than those created on the first and second weavings.

Assembling and Mounting

When all three weavings are completed, they are joined by stitching a tassel cord from the first and second weavings to the outside edges of the third (bottom) weaving (see fig. 7-27). Assemble so that the top edge of the bottom weaving just meets the bottom edges of the other two pieces. Grey wool which matches the wrapping on the fringes is used so that the stitching will be invisible against the wrapped cord. Small yarn loops added to the backs of the top two weavings will permit hanging without adding a hard, alien mounting bar to such a soft-textured work.

You might consider adding additional pieces to the work, using the same or an alternate design sequence. "Steps" could grow over the years to cover an entire wall.

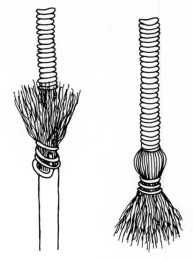

Fig. 7-32   Wrapping the tassels.

DESIGN

LEARNING DESIGN

More and more exceptional artists are turning up who are self-taught, with a degree in English or plumbing. Although a list of fine art academies looks terrific on a resumé, many would-be innovative artists are inhibited by an art school background that has been too strict. Just as the child who is reprimanded for drawing a green cow becomes afraid to trust in and experiment with his perceptions of things, so, too, does the adult whose teacher has become preoccupied with producing a specific result, rather than teaching technique and allowing for individual interpretation. How much more interesting it is to see fifteen different interpretations of a landscape ranging from mediocre to good, than to see a group of excellent works which are exact replicas of an instructor's. I once dropped out of a pottery course because of an instructor's rigidity. She refused to let me use a brown glaze on the inside of a bowl I'd made, saying brown glaze was unappetizing and could not be used on an eating vessel!

One must also use judgment in learning from a book. Lots of volumes will offer advice on how to judge a piece of artwork and list clearly what elements must be present to render a work "good." You can learn exactly where the central focus of a piece should be—and wind up totally intimidated in the process. What the books and some of the instructors don't tell you is that it's possible to break all the rules and still come up with a successful work of art.

One of the best ways to learn about art is to see it. Go to museums, visit galleries, scan library books showing artworks. Really examine a piece to understand why you find it pleasing, and ask yourself how it makes you feel. Be aware of how your eyes move through it; which elements dominate your attention, which carry you to another area, which lead you back into the body of the work. Try to discover why you feel drawn to certain kinds of work and determine how they relate to your own perceptions of various subjects.

Design in Nature

Look around you at the natural world—the best design is there. I look through my window at the frozen persimmons left clinging to the large tree. The leaves are long gone and the fruit remains; in clusters on some branches, in lines on others, in separate spheres on others. I am drawn to certain areas: in one, the persimmons seem to be huddled together, losing their individual shapes to become one, as though united against the coming storm. In another, they each remain perfect circles, leading one to another in a curve repeating their shapes, as though they willingly prepare for descent. The natural world can teach us all we need to know about design.

All around me, in nature, I find the principles I try to convey in my own works: rhythm, balance, emphasis, unity, and simplicity. I find rhythm in the bark of the black walnut tree and in the woodpecker holes in it. Each line travels to another, repeating the same theme in slightly different ways, leading into and out of new structures, amusing and delighting my eyes. I see balance in the mushroom clusters and in the fronds of the fern. My attention is not drawn to merely one side of the plant; it is dispersed and carried from one place to another. I find unity in my cat's fur. Swirling stripes and spots of grey, brown, and black, heavy pronounced lines and subtle receding ones, all create the pattern that he wears. Many elements are present, but they don't conflict with each other; instead they work together to create design. I see emphasis in the rusty gold of the dahlia blossom. The petals repeat themselves and continue in colors and shapes, but I return again and again to the center of the flower, to the richly colored part, the tightly closed, strong protruding eye of the plant which the rest of the flower gently echoes. I find simplicity and a color lesson in the most brightly painted butterfly who wears well an outfit we would think quite gaudy. But the butterfly is never overly decorated, colors project and recede, blending in flight to create new ones. The wing design shows

Fig. 8-1 Design experiments with paper and nails. (Arranged by Jennifer Philippoff)

clearly that nothing need be added or subtracted to improve him. Look closely at anything in nature and you will find these principles operating in harmony.

Design Experiments

An interesting method of experimenting with design is to cut pieces of paper in geometrical or free-form shapes and to manipulate them to form different patterns (fig. 8-1). Stop to see what you like or don't like about each design before moving on to create new ones. A friend of mine teaches his sculpture class to experiment with design in much the same way. He has students pour cut nails from a cup, arrange them, collect them, and pour again. It's often more comfortable to begin designing with familiar materials than with the materials of a new medium.

Another valid and valuable way to learn design is to create small pieces with a fiber technique and move them into various positions before assembling them. With macrame and wrapping it is especially easy to experiment by taking a long piece of

the work, a half knot sinnet, for example, and draping it over or through other parts of the work to see
how its movement affects other areas of the piece,
before securing it.

Preliminary Sketches

Many artists sketch their ideas or a portion of a
work before executing it. This can be valuable to an
extent, but, as I learned last year, it can also be det-
rimental. As exhibition director for an art center, I
organized a multimedia show entitled "Visions and
Revisions," which called for submission of a preliminary sketch and a model or maquet along with
each finished piece. The show was interesting but
disappointing, too, because many of the preliminary works were better than the final pieces. I won-
dered about this and then realized that most of
these pieces had failed because the artist had
strictly adhered to the original drawing of the work
and paid no heed to the special demands and possibilities of his or her medium. Some potentially
beautiful fiberworks looked terrific on paper but
failed miserably because they were made of linen
or wool and not graphite and paper. A medium and
an artist must have a constant rapport and dialogue
throughout a piece, or the struggle of the artist to
over-control becomes grossly evident. Keep in
mind, then, that a preliminary drawing can be useful as a rough idea only; your work will undoubtedly
want to move in another direction or depart from
your drawing at some point, and you must be prepared to let it do so.

Sometimes midway through a work a second
design is born of the one you're in the process of
executing and it's just too late to change the work
to portray the new and better idea. Frustration and
excitement mingle. I usually find it best to continue
the current work and treat it as a preliminary one,
leading to the new expression. The learning process is really what is most important and each new
work will undoubtedly teach you something more
than its precursors.

Recording Inspirations

Inspirations will come from everywhere when you
open yourself to them. They'll come from parts of
works you've seen, as vivid images that remain with

you long after you've forgotten where you saw the work. They'll come from the physical world around you. They'll come as you work on the fiber pieces themselves. Each inspiration should be recorded in a notebook with a verbal description or perhaps a rough sketch to remind you of it when you are ready to bring the idea to fruition. If you have an interest in photography, a photo journal can be especially helpful. Perhaps a piece of architecture particularly impressed you—a photo will help you see it vividly again before creating a fiber structure based on it. A catalog of nature photography will be important, too, when the seasons change and the fungi or ice formations you want to interpret are no longer available for reference.

INSPIRATION FROM NATURE

Earth Formations

Earth formations—mountains, valleys, rock layers, ice structures, and land patterns—are frequently reflected in tapestry weavings and other fiber media. Plowed fields and tall grasses in muted greens and browns form designs when seen from a distance, and their simple abstract lines are easily recreated in a fiberwork. Massive stalactites seen some time ago in a cave in Virginia remain in my mind and in my journal. One day I will create an environment based on them, so large that one will be able to step through it, but I must wait until I have a studio large enough to accommodate it. One day while glancing through a book on animal habitats, I was struck by a drawing of a fox's burrow and its strange resemblance to the cave sculpture. "Vixen's Earth" grew out of a combination of both ideas, an exercise in fiberwork and in patience. "Secret Garden" (see fig. 4-10) followed "Vixen's Earth" (fig. 4-6) and, as a three-dimensional work, is the predecessor for the stalactites I will wrap some day. Crystal formations pictured in an old magazine remind me that a weaving in subtle shades of white and grey will eventually echo them in my work.

Plant Life

All forms of plant life—flowers, seed pods, vines, fungi, even common green peppers—can serve as ideas for fiberwork. An evening spent among the

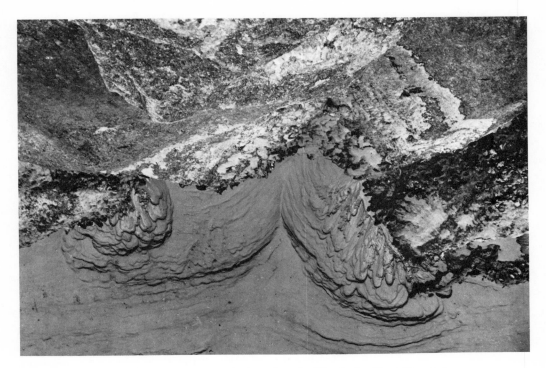

Fig. 8-2 Amorphous patterns in mud-glazed rock. (Photo by Paul Maurer)

Fig. 8-3 Sculptural forms within a green pepper.

cypress roots of a Mississippi swamp still remains in my mind. Two years later I was working on "Ocean Springs Life," a piece incorporating many fiber methods, in hopes of expressing both the feelings and the rich images I experienced among the cypress.

Animals and Their Creations

The works of our natural artisans are, of course, magnificent subjects as well. Nests, tunnels, hives, and webs have all been interpreted in fiber pieces. "Metamorphosis," a knotted and wrapped work (see fig. 8-28), has a pouch that hardly resembles an egg case, and the feathers dancing on the wrapped jute don't really look like insects. Yet the feelings of change and hatching are there, and the work is more eloquent for not being a literal interpretation. A goat mask with antique shoe-scraper horns is not immediately recognizable as a goat, perhaps, but it has a personality that goat lovers can identify. Butterfly wings will arise from my silken warp threads one day along with designs based on the fantastic shell patterns of East Asian beetles.

The Sea and Sky

Let the sea and all its plant and animal life advise you. In a single visit to the ocean I envisioned the lethal beauty of a dying jellyfish in a sculptural crochet with long tentacles dangling from it, and saw the bird claw patterns in the sand as a long and narrow pictographic weaving. I saw the rosy spiral patterns of the pear welk in a coiled piece of smooth cottons and silk, the curving lines of shells and spume left by receding waves in an abstract macrame work of heavy knotted bars between open floating cords.

Sunrise, sunset, clouds, stars, lightning, and thunder are all well-known subjects in traditional American Indian art. They can influence our work as well, appearing as bold designs or subtle expressions.

Natural Found Objects

You can collect bones, shells, and nuts to heighten a fiber statement or design a work specifically to complement them. Often the shape of a

Fig. 8-4   Wing designs of the monarch butterfly. (Photo by Paul Maurer)

Fig. 8-5   A hornet's nest—geometric and free-form sculpture combined.

Fig. 8-6   The spirals and spatial and linear designs of seashells.

Fig. 8-7 Billowy cloud formations against the undulat-
ing earth. (Photo by Paul
Reid)

gnarled or twisted branch or perhaps a burl forma-
tion on the wood (fig. 8-8) will be the only inspiration needed for a piece. A friend, an avid hiker,
collects animal skulls she finds in the forest and
creates masks directly on them, supporting her
fiber with a natural armature and using exposed
bone as part of the design.

INSPIRATION FROM THE MANMADE WORLD
History

The Swiss psychologist Carl Jung spoke of a
"collective unconscious." He said that within each
of us there is a record of all man's past unconscious experience and that we catch fleeting
glimpses of it as it becomes progressively buried in
the refuse of modern civilization. I tend to believe in
this collective unconscious experience when I see
a contemporary fiberwork and then find an ancient
museum piece unknown to the modern fiber artist
but so similar that the pieces are almost duplicates
of each other. It also happens sometimes that two
artists in different parts of the world produce strik-
ingly similar, complicated pieces, each without
knowing of the other work. Two things are certain:

we are related to all humankind, and our collective history can be incredibly inspirational.

Ancient peoples, their rituals, gods, and demons, are an important source of imagery for my work. I feel the power of another's belief when I read of shaman, fetishes, and ceremonial masks and can embrace and be moved by our shared quest for a spiritual world even as I keep my own religious beliefs.

Other cultures such as the Egyptians, Druids, ancient Japanese, and Incas all call forth ideas for fiberworks. Fiber-sculpted architectural forms, weavings with pictographic symbols dancing through them, and knotted masks personifying legends and ideals can all be inspired by historical studies.

Greek mythology is full of characters to portray, stories to interpret, images to convey. "Jason's Prize," a wool and goat hair interpretation of the golden fleece, hangs in my studio. "Medusa," a mask with snakelike wire-reinforced wrapped hair, spanning over four feet, waits in my notebook along with a monumental piece—Pandora's box. Folklore from around the world, especially British nursery rhymes, are favorite subjects to interpret anew. The simple rhymes we recited as children were not so innocent, I learn as an adult. "Ring Around the Roses," it seems, was really about the widespread death resulting from the plague. I envision expressing my new knowledge of the rhyme and the feelings I harbor about childhood misconceptions in a crochet work.

Recent history, too, can be motivational. Factual history can be recorded, patriotism expressed, and political statements voiced in fiber forms.

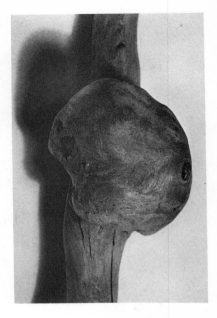

Fig. 8-8 The strange grain patterns and form of a burl growth.

Personal and Psychological Statements

Humor is often expressed in a fiber medium, as are fantasy and sometimes biting satire. After an exhausting day of examining fiber portfolios for possible inclusion in this book, and having just been through several artists' work who dealt with very lofty subjects, I came across a work that was delightful in its humor, satire, and simplicity. It consisted of several brown stuffed woven forms which curled around and over each other to create a

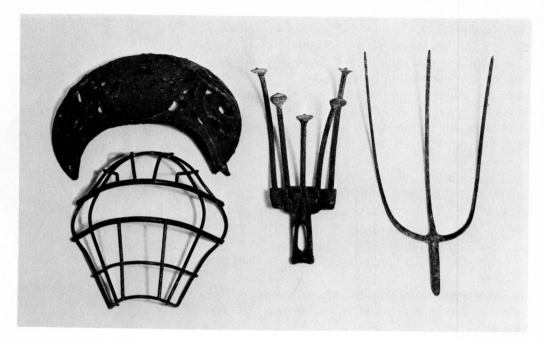

Fig. 8-9 Found tools with hollows, curves, and antler-like projections.

sculpture. (Perhaps I should have included this piece in "Animals and their Creations"!)

The whole range of human emotion can be expressed in fiber. Love, fury, isolation, and all the nuances of feeling inbetween can be presented through form, technique, color, and texture.

One can convey an entire family history through weaving alone. There are fiber artists who portray likenesses of relatives in their work by referring to photographs as they weave. Incorporating heirlooms in a piece or using a family antique as a basis for a work is another way to convey a personal statement.

Manmade Found Objects

Found objects, whether they be inherited, bought, or plucked from someone's trash bin, can enhance a work and also prove to be sources of ideas. Often an old farm implement or just part of an implement will have such an interesting linear design that you will be moved to create a work based solely on repeating the curves and hollows of the metal. Sometimes the fiberworks come first and the tools are added to help express an idea, but I always examine new found objects carefully, turning them in all directions to give them a chance to speak for themselves and indicate whether they are to be a primary or secondary focus in a work. An animal trap can be used as a base for a fiberwork whose subject is wildlife protection, or it can be employed for its aesthetic beauty totally disregarding its function. A piece of barn door hardware with a large turning wheel inspired a knotted work with repetitive circular themes entitled "Wheel of Fortune" (see fig. 8-10). An old curved scale bed, resembling a huge oval seed pod, received coiled and crocheted work which seems to be sprouting from it. Any type of found object, metal or non-metal (old barrel rings, wooden hames, chair legs, etc.), can be used in your work and lead to new types of expression.

A FIBER ARTS GALLERY

The photographs on the following pages show how several artists have used macrame, wrapping, coiling, crochet, and weaving, often combining several media in one work, to transform their inspirations into fiber art.

Fig. 8-11 "Forest Shrine." Anne Dushanko-Dobek. 28" x 41" x 4". This nature-inspired work is composed of single crochet and variations of single crochet. The artist evokes a sense of mystery by contrasting large forms with groups of smaller ones. (Photo courtesy of the artist)

Fig. 8-10 "Wheel of Fortune." Author. 1' x 4'. The piece of barn door hardware from which it hangs inspired this macrame work.

Fig. 8-12 "Winter Bloom." Ruth Gowell. 21" diameter. One of a series of flower-inspired coiled and woven baskets. The looped lid lifts off to disclose a secret compartment. (Photo courtesy of the artist)

Fig. 8-13 "Jeune Afrique." Carol Lukitsch. 32″ x 40″. A burnt wood mounting bar supports the pouch-like structure of the crocheted and coiled work. (Photo by Marilyn Grelle)

Fig. 8-14 "Mayan." Patricia McKenna Glavé. 4′ x 4′ x 1′. Rows of clove hitches form projecting shapes in this work, inspired by the bas relief sculptures of the Yucatan ruins. (Photo courtesy of the artist)

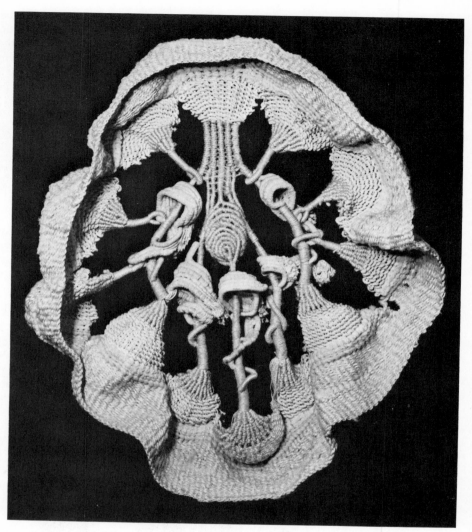

Fig. 8-15 "Untitled." Carol Beron. 5' diameter. This fungus- and flower-inspired progression of forms shows a dramatic use of positive and negative spaces. The artist used wrapping, coiling, twining, and knotting. (Photo courtesy of the artist)

Fig. 8-16 "Soft Birthday Cake." Ruth Geneslaw. 13" x 13". Weaving, crochet, and wrapping were employed to create this whimsical sculpture. (Photo by Michael Smirnoff)

Fig. 8-17 "Paul and Me." Anne Mitchell. 4" x 4". A woven family portrait.

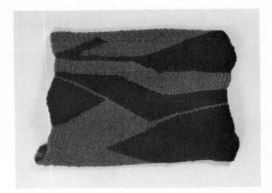

Fig. 8-18 "Northern Pillar." Renata McElroy. 11" x 8". This work was inspired by Navajo weaving techniques and designs. By mounting the flat work on a metal armature the artist has created a relief sculpture. (Photo courtesy of the artist)

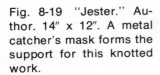

Fig. 8-19 "Jester." Author. 14" x 12". A metal catcher's mask forms the support for this knotted work.

Fig. 8-20 "Birth Control Baby." Susan Aaron-Taylor. 17" × 13" × 7". The artist has used coiling techniques and an assembled construction to make her social statement. (Photo by Harry Wm. Taylor)

Fig. 8-21. "Birth Control Baby" disassembled. (Photo by Harry Wm. Taylor)

Fig. 8-22 "Primitif." Carol Lukitsch. 21" x 8'. Composed on a steel ring armature, this work contains elements of crochet and wrapping. (Photo by Spectrum)

Fig. 8-23 "Gargoyle." Patricia McKenna Glavé. 2' x 6' x 1'. Inspired by medieval sculptures, the distorted face of this knotted and wrapped work resembles that of a gothic gargoyle. (Photo courtesy of the artist)

Fig. 8-24 "Horse Feathers." Author. 3' x 5'. An antique horse hame supports this work, composed of a combination of macrame techniques.

Fig. 8-25 "Siamese." Patricia McKenna Glavé. 3' x 6' x 1¹/₂'. Wrapped appendages protrude from the center of this large knotted work. The artist used the textures of the clove hitch and the reverse side of the clove hitch when folding and building the bold sculptural forms. (Photo courtesy of the artist)

Fig. 8-26 "Bomblies." Susan Aaron-Taylor. 1½' x 3'. Sculptural crochet and weaving combine to give this nature-inspired work a whimsical look. (Photo by Harry Wm. Taylor)

Fig. 8-27 "Miniature Rainbow Landscape." Ruth Geneslaw. 12" x 25". Wrapped elements surround a tapestry landscape; other sections of this work are crocheted and woven. (Photo courtesy of the artist)

Fig. 8-28 "Metamorphosis." Author. 4' x 5'. The image of a cocoon with insects hatching out is suggested in this clove hitch knotted and wrapped work.

HANDSPINNING

In this world of modern technology and instant everything, there is a special joy to be found in journeying with an idea from its conception to completion and being personally involved in every step of its maturation. If planting a simple vegetable garden can renew our faith in our self-sufficiency, imagine what taking the fleece from a sheep, spinning it into yarn, giving it color from our garden and transforming it into an artwork can do for us. Surely it's faster and much easier to sit at your desk and mail order yarn in an array of colors. It's easier to buy a tomato in a store too, but you miss the pleasure of tending it and watching it grow. There is something magical that happens; images of fairy-tale characters and ancient peoples flow through your mind as you spin and witness the birth of the yarn you'll spend hours working with and years enjoying in its final form. The handspinning process is neither mysterious nor difficult and requires only time and a few simple tools (fig. 9-2).

Fig. 9-1 Woolgathering. (Photo by Christopher Leaman)

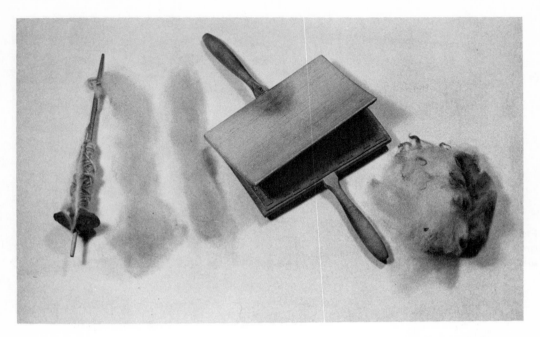

Fig. 9-2 The spindle, rolags, cards, and fleece with which handspun yarn is created.

OBTAINING AND PREPARING THE WOOL

Wool is about the best material with which to begin handspinning because its length and texture make it easier to handle than other types of fibers. Different breeds of sheep give different types of wool. The long silky fleece of the Corriedale and Cheviot breeds are excellent for spinning a medium-coarse yarn. For finer yarns, the soft fleece of the Merino is recommended. You can buy wool already carded, or cleaned and carded, from weaving supply houses, or go directly to the farm to obtain it. If you go to the farm, you will no doubt be purchasing it "in the grease," that is, uncleaned, with the natural lanolin of the animal still in it (fig. 9-3). When picking from fleece of various qualities, it is important to look for wool that is fairly clean with long, soft, fine locks and a moist grease in it. Certain sections of wool which covered the underside of the sheep will be excessively dirty and coarse and should be avoided. Fleece that is matted or whose natural oil has dried and hardened will be weak and next to impossible to card and spin. Most spinners prefer to work with unwashed fleece because the oils aid in the spinning process. If you store large quantities of wool in the grease be sure to keep it in a moisture-free place and in a porous

Fig. 9-3 Raw fleece "in the grease" before removal of twigs and burrs.

or open container since the natural oils can be combustible.

Teasing

The first step in preparing the wool for spinning is teasing the fleece. Taking a small handful of wool, gently remove a piece of it, and spread it from one hand to another, gently separating and fluffing the fibers without pulling the piece apart. Seeds, burrs, and twigs can be removed at this time and loose dirt will fall to your lap.

Carding

Combing or carding is the next step. Carding continues the separation and cleansing of the teased fleece and aligns the fibers for spinning. Wool carders can be purchased at a weaving supply house or you can improvise with wire-toothed dog brushes. A weaver friend who lives as close to nature as possible uses the seed helmets of dried wild teasel plants to card her fibers in the manner of the early settlers. Begin the carding process by evenly applying a small teased lock of fleece to the card or brushes and pulling each card over the other with a brushing motion (fig. 9-4). The wool should be shifted from one card to the other as the cards are pulled lightly to straighten and arrange the fibers in parallel order.

Shorter animal hair can be added during the carding process to produce a varigated yarn. Some

Fig. 9-4 Carding the wool.

spinners desiring a less evenly spun yarn will spin
teased fleece and omit the carding.

When the fleece is thoroughly carded, it should
be gently freed from the card and rolled into a thin
long tube of parallel fibers called a rolag (see fig.
9-2). You should prepare several rolags to have
close at hand because many of them will be used to
spin each cone of yarn.

DROP SPINNING

The Drop Spindle

The common drop spindle is made of a piece of
tapered wood about a foot long, with a thin disc or
whorl near the bottom of its shank and a notch at
the top (fig. 9-5). Spindles can be either purchased
or fashioned from dowels and door knobs, Yo-Yo
halves, or ceramic discs. The spindle rotates like a

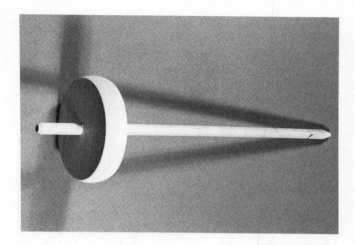

Fig. 9-5   A drop spindle.

top, spinning and twisting the fibers attached to it to form the yarn. The whorl continues the spin of the shaft and acts as a weight, pulling the fibers into a strand as they are spun.

Dressing the Spindle

A piece of yarn, approximately a yard long and called the leader, is fastened to the spindle shaft just above the whorl (disc). The yarn is wound around the spindle several times before it is brought down over the edge of the whorl, around the shaft tip, back over the whorl, and up the shaft to the notch (fig. 9-6). A half hitch fastens the yarn to the notch, leaving an end of yarn several inches long to which the fleece fibers will be joined to begin the spinning process.

Spinning the Yarn

Spinning is begun by twisting a few of the rolag fibers onto the leader end and giving the spindle a clockwise spin (the spindle dangles in the air). Pull down on the rolag with the thumb and forefingers of one hand, twisting the spindle when necessary and letting the spin twist the fleece. The other hand should be used to hold the rolag fibers in a V shape to feed into the spinning yarn (fig. 9-7). When the spindle has spun a length of yarn and is nearing the floor, it's time to wind the yarn onto the shank of the spindle before continuing the spinning process. Experiment with your spinning at first, giving a rapid spin to the shank to produce a tightly

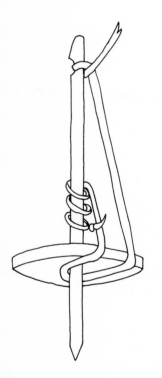

Fig. 9-6   Dressing the spindle.

Fig. 9-7 Spinning with the drop spindle.

twisted cord or turning it more slowly to create a loftier yarn.

Other types of spindles you might like to investigate include the Navaho spindle or beedizi and the Turkish spindle. The Navaho is a large spindle that is supported against the leg with the spindle shank touching the floor or ground. It is used to spin long coarse fibers forming a heavy yarn. The Turkish spindle resembles a smaller version of the drop spindle and is used to create a fine yarn (from silken threads, for instance).

NATURAL DYES

Using plant material to dye yarn and fabrics or to produce body stain is an ancient art that has been practiced worldwide for thousands of years. The Aztecs used poinsettia and wild dahlia for their garments, indigo was used in ancient Asia, and lichens were employed by the Scots. People in diverse cultures experimented with and perfected the use of available dye plants, passing their recipes to successive generations. The colors were both muted or brilliant; the fabrics and yarns quite colorfast.

Natural dyes were the only coloring agents available until the 1800s when a mauve-colored coal tar substance was discovered which marked the beginning of the chemical dye industry. The old plant dye recipes fell by the wayside as mass produced commercial dyes took over. Colors could now be exactly duplicated—another boon for civilization, or so it seemed. The renaissance of natural dyes in the past few years has opened many an eye to colors rarely seen before, except perhaps on museum tapestries and in the garden. The subtle and rich hues which dye plants impart delight our eyes and give us a feeling of tranquility that is impossible to find in frenzied hot pinks and electric blues.

FINDING DYE PLANTS

City dwellers as well as country folk will find natural dyestuffs close at hand. Gathering dyestuffs is not difficult; most every kitchen contains several dye pigments already. Tea, coffee, onion skins, and spinach can all produce a coloring bath. Early man probably discovered natural dyes in the stains on his skin produced by plant juices. Like him, we've all done some accidental natural dying; unlike him, we usually spend a great deal of time trying to remove the stain instead of experimenting further with it.

Outdoors lies a boundless source of dyestuffs. Bark, roots, berries, nuts, flowers (wild and cultivated), mosses, weeds, and roots all contain some coloring pigment that we can use in the dyebath. Imported seeds have given us an even wider choice of dye plants than available to ancient man, who could only use what was at hand in his immediate environment.

Dyestuffs in the Wild

Several bags for collecting plant material, some scissors for taking cuttings, a notebook to record the place and time of collecting, and, perhaps, a pocket guide to wildflowers, grasses, and trees are all you'll need for your first collecting excursion. Once afield, you'll probably wish you had your camera and binoculars, too, but go unencumbered the first time. After you see first hand the colors natural dyes can impart, you'll be making plenty of enjoyable trips to the field.

Field Flowers. A short walk to a field near my home in suburban Pennsylvania provides several dyestuffs. Those of you who live in the country will have even greater access to wildflowers and grasses. In that one small unmown field, however, I find fennel, a prolific member of the carrot family, and knotweed, another prolific plant of the buckwheat family. Both give me a mustard yellow or brown dye. I also find goldenrod for tans and oranges and milkweed for moss green and yellow-green yarn. Crown vetch, which grows in profusion along the nearby roadsides, covers a good portion of the field and provides more turquoise green than I could possibly use. Butterflies soar by, flashing wing colors I'll never achieve and leading me to the butterfly weed, source of orange, green, and brown dyes. Yarrow waits nearby to give me yellows; coreopsis imparts a beautiful red-orange to the dyebath.

The bees scold for a moment—I am interrupting their work as I look around at the color combinations in the flower heads, feeling the sun upon my back. Once again the tranquility of nature fills me and I realize that if the flowers collected produced no color at all, my time spent here would be worth my trouble. But produce color they will, not the same shades as the year before or even the day before, but new colors, just as beautiful or even more beautiful because each new shade is a discovery.

Berries. The blackberries and elderberries form a ring around the field, imparting purples to my fingers and grey-blues and greys to the yarns I dye with them. Poke berries, which ripen a little later, will rival the beautiful reds achieved with madder. The dye will fade a bit, but become more beautiful, I believe, in the process.

Trees. The distinctive mitten-shaped leaves of the sassafras tree remind me that soothing tea and rosy-brown dye await me in its roots. I don't usually like to use the roots of a plant, but I've been told, and it seems true from experience, that for each sassafras dug, two grow back in its place. Once you've got sassafras, it seems, you've got it for keeps. I find brown and black dyes inside black walnut hulls, and lichens, which grow on the oak tree, surprise me again and again with magentas and oranges they hide within their drab disguise.

Garden Flowers. Across the street, tucked into the hillside lies "Cockelbur," a log house built in the 1600s. All around it trails garden after garden, filled with fragrant dyestuffs. A remarkable woman lives here, as strong and interesting as the dwelling in which she lives. Mildred Erdman loves the wild and cultivated flowers, herbs, and flowering trees and tends them well. The flowers, in turn, grow exceedingly lush and beautiful, and I expect her annuals return a second year just to see her. The flowers delight my senses, fill my camera frame, and when they grow too crowded or blossoms begin to fade, they fill my dyepots to winter in another form.

Daffodils and chrysanthemums provide gold and yellow dyes; the plump dahlia blossoms give orange. The delicate lupine and the purple foxglove supply varying shades of green, while the dark blue hyacinth imparts a pale blue to my wools. Shades of brown I find in sumac leaves, especially easy to use as they contain tannin, a natural mordant. I'll stop here, although Mildred's gardens bear at least two dozen more dye plants, out of sympathy for city dwellers who have no roof to garden.

Drying Plants for Future Use. Many dye plants can be dried and saved for future use (fig. 10-1). Using dried plants is not as aromatic an experience as dyeing with them fresh and certainly not as much of a visual pleasure, but it still beats mail-or-

dering them. Some plant material, such as bark, roots, and lichen, which are rich in natural mordants, retain their full dye potential when dried, but most plants will give paler shades if not used fresh. Moldy dyestuffs or flowers which have faded drastically will give little or no color. For this reason, to save them for future dyebaths, plants must be air dried slowly and carefully and then stored in jars in a dry, dark place.

Dyes from Foods

Whether country dweller or not, everyone has access to a grocery store. The produce department of your local supermarket can provide you with plenty of dyestuffs, yielding a wide range of colors (fig. 10-2). If you can develop a rapport with the produce manager, you will be amazed and delighted at the amount of scrap vegetation he can gather for you in a week. The dark outer leaves of the purple cabbage, for instance, will yield a striking range of blues, lavenders, and purples in the dyebath. Yellow onion skins will provide yellows and bronzy tans, while red skins will give rusty reds or greens. The skins and seeds of the pomegranate impart a yellow-orange color to unmordanted yarns, while beets will yield magenta and sometimes deep red.

A favorite white muslin dress has become my testing sheet for food dyes. Every time I wear it, the perverse imp who lives within me has a heyday. Coffee and tea streak down the front of it, while blackberry pie and grape juice mark the sleeves.

Fig. 10-2 Some of the many dye-yielding foods.

Tomato sauce has landed in my lap along with chocolate cake. Shall I bleach it mercilessly or embroider over it? A resounding "No!" These are not stains, but natural dyes, and the dress a growing piece of dyer's art. Try any food or plant material in the dyebath; most will yield some color, and perhaps you will discover a new source or rediscover an old, forgotten source for natural dye.

Dyes from Supply Houses

I can't believe if you've read this far you would actually prefer to buy dried, pre-packaged plant material rather than forage for it yourself. Still, I suppose, if you live in Alaska, are reading this in the dead of winter, or really want to use a plant that is unavailable in your neck of the woods or non-woods, you should know that plant materials are readily available through weaving supply and botanical supply houses (see Suppliers). In addition, there are some colors, notably clear blue and true red, that are just about impossible to achieve using plants native to the United States. For these colors, you will need to buy an exotic dye from a supplier—probably at exotic prices, too. Brilliant reds can be obtained with Asian madder roots and Mexican cochineal. The latter is composed of the dried bodies of tiny beetles, each insect providing a droplet of dye. I would sooner forego the cochineal than use a dye for which insects must be killed. Deep blue can be obtained by dying with the exotic indigo, and shades of red and blue will be achieved with imported logwood chips.

But it's much more educational, inspirational, and just plain fun to get out and collect dyestuffs yourself, rather than wait for the mailperson to deliver a dried clump of them.

THE DYEING PROCESS

Dyeing raw yarn with plant matter consists of three main steps: scouring or washing the yarn, mordanting the yarn so it will take the color, and dyeing. Methods vary depending upon individual choice and what kinds of fibers are to be dyed. Because wool takes color readily and is fairly easy to work with, it is advisable to use wool for your beginning experiments with natural dyes, moving on to other fibers as you become more experienced in dyepot technique. You can experiment on your own or gain information on dyeing silk, linen, or cotton from any of several books devoted to the subject.

Equipment

> Several large (5 or 6 gallon) dye or mordant pots, made of unchipped enamel or stainless steel
> Stirring rods, either glass or painted wood
> Measuring spoons, either plastic or stainless steel
> Rinsing buckets, either enamel or plastic
> Postal scale
> Rubber gloves

Glass, stainless, or enamel tools are strongly recommended because any metals present in equipment will react in the bath and cause color changes. This equipment list includes only the basic tools; others may be added as your dyeing knowledge progresses. Perhaps you'll want to add an iron or copper kettle to your supplies and enjoy the colors obtained as the natural mordants in the metals react with your dyes. On the other hand, you may in time decide to do without some of the measuring devices, estimating quantities and adding unweighed skeins of yarn to an approximate amount of plant material. Some people cannot be

Fig. 10-3 Scouring and mordanting agents used to prepare the wool for dyeing.

bothered by measuring plant and yarn quantities exactly and produce beautiful dyed yarns by estimating. In the beginning, however, it's best to follow directions carefully to avoid discouraging results.

Washing the Wool

If wool is purchased "pre-washed" you may skip the washing step. If it has not been previously washed, or is fresh from the spindle and still in the grease, the oils must be removed so that the mordant and dye solutions can penetrate the yarn. Wind your yarn into $1/2$-pound skeins (around your hand and elbow works fine) and tie it loosely in several places with cotton string. It is best to soak the wool in water overnight to thoroughly wet the fibers. In the morning submerge it in several gallons of lukewarm water to which 3 ounces of soap flakes have been added. If your water is excessively hard, a water softener should be added, or rainwater should be collected and used for the washing process. Handle the wool carefully, gently squeezing the suds through it, to avoid matting the fibers. Never twist or wring wool or expose it to sudden temperature changes as this will shock the fibers and cause the wool to become harsh.

After the wool is scoured, rinse it in lukewarm water until all the soap is removed. The wool should be lifted from the rinsing bucket and excess water squeezed from it before drying it in the shade. Washed yarn may also be stored wet in a plastic bag or jar if it is to be used in a few days, or it may be mordanted immediately if the mordant bath is ready.

Mordanting

A mordant is a chemical used before, during, or after the dyebath to bring out color and to make the dye more permanent. Some plant materials such as oak galls, sumac leaves, and staghorn moss contain natural mordants, and these dye materials may be used directly on washed unmordanted wool. Most natural dyes, however, do need the action of a chemical agent to fix them. Alum, chrome, copper, iron, and tin are some of the common mordants (see table 10-1), and each will produce a different shade of yarn even through used with the same coloring bath. Most dyers agree that the best and most permanent dyes are achieved by mordanting the yarn before it is dyed.

Mordanting must be done carefully with thoroughly wetted wool. Often one is tempted, as no visible change takes place in the mordant pot, to assume that shortcuts taken won't make much difference. When the mordanted yarn emerges from the dyeing solution, however, the quality of the mordanting becomes quite obvious as the tell-tale streaking of poorly mordanted wool is very visible.

Your mordanting supplies should include an exhaust fan if you're not working outside (some mordanting fumes are not healthy—see table 10-1) and cream of tartar (available at any grocery store), which helps distribute the mordant evenly through the yarn.

Table 10-1 COMMON MORDANTS

Mordant	Chemical name	Toxicity	Source
Alum	Aluminum potassium sulfate (granules or powder)	Nontoxic	Pharmacy or photo supply
Chrome	Potassium dichromate granules	Caustic and poisonous	Chemical or photo supply
Copper	Copper sulfate (blue vitriole)	Very toxic (use an unlined copper pot instead if possible)	Chemical supply
Iron	Ferrous sulfate (green vitriole or copperas)	Nontoxic	Chemical supply
Tin	Stannous chloride crystals	Toxic	Chemical supply

Mordanting with Alum. The following mordant instructions are for 1 pound of scoured wool.

    4 gallons soft water
    3 ounces alum
    1 ounce cream of tartar

Fill a stainless steel or enamel pot with about 4 gallons of cold, soft water and heat to lukewarm. Dissolve the alum and cream of tartar in a small amount of boiling water and add the solution to the pot of water. Add the thoroughly wetted wool to the mordant bath using wooden or glass rods. Gradually increase the heat of the water until it is just simmering (this should take about 30 minutes). Allow the wool to simmer for about 1 hour, turning and lifting it occasionally to distribute the mordant evenly. The wool should never boil and must be submerged throughout this process; if too much water evaporates during mordanting, lift the wool out, add more water to the pot and return the yarn to the bath.

When the yarn has simmered for an hour, turn off the heat and let the pot slowly cool. When the wool is cool enough to handle, gently squeeze the water from it, rinse it in water of the same temperature and allow it to dry, store it wet, or proceed directly to the dye bath.

Mordanting with Chrome. Chrome is more difficult to use than alum because it is sensitive to light and requires extra care to ensure good results. It is also a toxic chemical, producing potentially harmful fumes and should only be used in a well-ventilated area, preferably outdoors. Like all poisons, it must be kept out of the reach of children and animals and labeled as poison if it is transferred to another container. Still, the deep rich colors achieved with chrome make the difficulties involved in working with it well worth enduring.

For 1 pound of wool, use:

4 gallons soft water
$1/2$ ounce chrome

The mordanting procedure for chrome is the same as that for mordanting with alum, except that the above precautions must be taken and the mordanting pot must be covered. Chrome reacts with light and both the mordant bath and the wool taken from it must be shielded from light until the actual dyeing is done. A dark-colored plastic bag is good for storing the yarn in if you aren't dyeing it immediately.

Mordanting with Copper. Copper sulfate is highly toxic, and an alternative to its use is to dye the wool in an unlined copper pot. But for those undaunted by toxic substances, to mordant 1 pound of wool, use:

4 gallons soft water
$1/2$ ounce copper sulfate
1 ounce cream of tartar

Prepare the mordant solution and add the wetted wool to it, as described for mordanting with alum, but take the precautions necessary for working with chrome.

Bring the mordant bath to a simmer and allow to cook for 1 hour, lifting and moving the yarn to mordant evenly. Allow the solution to cool, rinse the yarn in water of the same temperature as the cooled bath, remove excess water and hang to dry, store wet, or dye.

Mordanting with Iron. For 1 pound of wool, use:

4 gallons soft water
$^1/_2$ ounce iron
$^1/_2$ ounce cream of tartar

Prepare the mordant solution carefully, because too much iron will harden the wool. Proceed as with alum mordanting.

Mordanting with Tin. When used as a mordant on undyed wool, tin tends to weaken the wool by making the fibers more brittle. But it has other uses—see Changing the Color after Dyeing, below.

Preparing Plant Material for Dyeing

In general, you will want to use twice the amount of plant material as yarn in your dye formulas. So for 4 ounces of wool, you would use about 8 ounces ($^1/_2$ pound) of dyestuff. Some flowers are less potent and will require a greater concentration of them to extract a good dye. Other flowers and plants, such as marigold and oxalis, will yield fine color if used in a one-to-one ratio (in weight) with wool. You can tear, crush, or chop flower petals and use them alone or with stems and leaves to achieve various shades of color. Break apart bits of bark and woody substances, grind or chop roots, and crush ripe berries to hasten the release of dye ooze. Remember to use stainless steel, glass, or wooden tools to avoid unexpected mordanting with other metals.

Preparing the Dyebath

Place the prepared plant material in a stainless steel, enamel, or glass pot, cover it with water, and let it stand overnight. In the morning, boil the mixture for 1$^1/_2$ to 2 hours depending upon the speed at which the dye is released from the plant. Strain the solution into the dye kettle (fig. 10-4), add about 4 gallons of cold water, or enough to cover your wet wool skeins without crowding, and heat the bath to lukewarm.

Dyeing, Rinsing, and Drying

Enter the thoroughly wetted wool skeins into the lukewarm dyebath, moving and lifting them, without actually stirring, to distribute the dye evenly. Slowly bring the lukewarm water to a simmer and

Fig. 10-4 Straining the dye ooze from logwood chips, a source of blue and purple dyes.

allow it to remain at this temperature for from 1/2 to 1 hour (up to 2 hours for barks and roots), moving the yarn back and forth occasionally to distribute the color evenly.

Remove your skeins of yarn from the dyepot and begin rinsing, starting with water that is the same temperature as the dyebath and continuing with slightly cooler rinses until the rinse water is clear. Then remove the wool and squeeze out excess moisture. You can roll the skeins in a towel, if you like, before hanging them to dry in the shade. Never put woolen skeins in a clothes dryer or hang them to dry in sunlight or near a heat source. These sudden temperature changes will damage the wool fibers.

An alternative method of dyeing, especially good if you plan to dye lesser amounts of wool, is to add the wet wool skeins directly to the broken-up plant material with just enough water to cover the wool. The entire mixture is then brought to a simmer, allowed to remain simmering for about 30 minutes, and cooled in the pot. The yarn then remains in the plant ooze overnight and is rinsed and dried the following day.

The dyebath may be cooled and stored in a labeled glass jar for several days if you wish to reuse it for lighter shades of color. Keep the dye in your refrigerator, if possible, as dyestuffs will spoil rapidly if they are kept at room temperature.

Changing the Color after Dyeing

Acid and Alkaline Rinses. If an acid or alkaline ingredient is added to the last rinse after dyeing, it will often intensify and sometimes completely change the color of a dyed yarn. Small amounts of white vinegar or lemon juice, both acids, will often turn blues to lavenders and further redden existing purples. A single teaspoonful of ammonia, an alkali, will often turn orangey hues to red. Yarns should, of course, be thoroughly rinsed again in plain water after treating them with alkaline or acid substances.

Top-Dyeing. You can change colors with which you are not satisfied (you must be very hard to please!) by top-dyeing, that is, entering the dyed yarn in another color dyebath. Using this process, you can also combine colors to create greens from yellow and blue solutions and turquoise from blues and greens, changing hues in various ways.

Using Tin as a Blooming Agent. Although somewhat difficult to employ as a mordant prior to dyeing because it tends to make wool brittle, tin works well when it is used on a premordanted yarn that has just been dyed. If used in this way, it brightens or blooms the color of the yarn, often turning yellows to orange and some browns to reddish colors. Use an exhaust fan if working indoors.

To act as a blooming agent on one pound of wool, tin is added as follows:

$1/2$ ounce tin crystals
$1/2$ ounce cream of tartar

Dissolve the tin in water and do the same with the cream of tartar. Remove the yarn from the dyebath and add both mixtures to the dyebath. Stir the new solution, put the wool back in, and simmer for 10 to 15 minutes. Remove the yarn and rinse it in a bath of soapy water of the same temperature as the bath from which it was taken. Follow this rinse with progressively cooler ones until the water runs clear.

Using Iron as a Saddening Agent. Adding iron and cream of tartar during the dyeing process improves color fastness and darkens or saddens the color, imparting muted tones to the yarn. Follow the directions for blooming with tin, but use iron salts instead. Simmering wool in an iron pot would also sadden the colors obtained in the dyebath.

Fermentation Dyeing

Fermentation dyeing consists of soaking or steeping an unmordanted yarn in a covered jar containing plant material and a mixture of water and either ammonia or stale urine. The plant material usually begins to ferment within a week, producing a dye liquor strong enough to color the yarn without simmering. Some dyers add a bit of the ooze to a dyebath and proceed with dyeing as usual, but the best results are achieved by placing the wool right in the jar with the fermenting dyestuffs. The steeping process is quite simple but requires patience, a warm place to store jars, and a willingness to experience some pretty strange odors at times. The resulting colors, however, are striking—even magentas can be obtained by fermenting lichens and roots. Some fermentation formulas appear below under Natural Dye Formulas.

DYER'S RECORDBOOK

Notebook entries made in the field and jotted down during mordanting and dyeing procedures can now be combined with a sample of the dyed yarn and kept in a book which will be a reference for you and inspiration for your would-be dyer friends (fig. 10-5). Entries should include the date, location of collection, and type of plant gathered. I find it helpful to make note of how many bags of plant material I collected and how abundant the supply of a particular dyestuff is in a particular location so that I may return there if I need a large bath of a certain dye. You may want to dry a small sample of a particularly unusual plant and staple this in a plastic bag to the recordbook page.

Keep track of mordanting and dyeing procedures and how much plant material you've used in each dyepot. Make note of any mistakes made, as they

Fig. 10-5   Page from a dyer's recordbook.

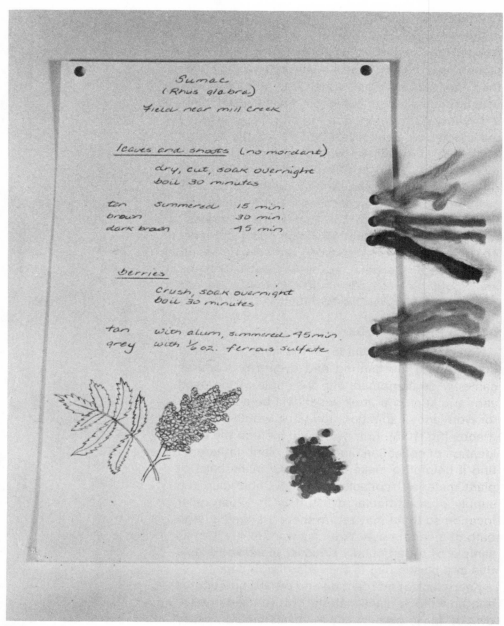

sometimes give delightful results and you'll want to remember how to produce similar colors in the future. I say "similar" because no two dye baths ever yield exactly the same color. Time of year, age of plant, and growing conditions all determine the dye properties of the plant. Add to this the subtle differences in wools and the human error factor and you've accumulated quite a set of variables. Hopefully you're not going to be bothered by slightly different color qualities in a group of wool skeins of the "same" color. Contrary to the instructions on commercial yarns, it really won't ruin a piece of work to have a slight difference in yarn hue—if anything, it adds to the piece. To stockpile yarns of exactly the same color, you'd have to dye with crown vetch in a vat over a bonfire—or, alas, use commercial dyes.

Samples of natural dyed yarn strung through holes punched in an oaktag page will not only look beautiful but will also remind you of the multitude of colors and shades obtainable (see color photo 5). Any information (whether the method of dyeing was easy or too time consuming, etc.) will be helpful to you and perhaps to another person with whom you share the records. I like to make a note about each collecting excursion as well, perhaps to bring bread for the ducks next time or that nettles prevent my bringing my dog along. Mention of the owl I saw in the tree or the farmer with whom I chatted give me a dyer's diary as well as a dyer's recordbook.

NATURAL DYE FORMULAS

The following dye formulas, prepared for 4 ounces of wool, will help you to begin working with natural dyes. When you have achieved results with these formulas, begin to experiment on your own to discover a limitless supply of natural colors for your fibers.

Dyes from Wild Plants
Goldenrod
> Locations found: Roadsides and fields in Canada and the United States.
> To prepare dye: Cover 1 pound of torn flowers with water and bring the water to a boil. Boil for 1 hour to extract the dye.

Fig. 10-6 Goldenrod.

Fig. 10-7 Coreopsis.

Fig. 10-8 Nightshade.

Fig. 10-9 Pigweed.

Strain out the solid matter and add enough water to cover the yarn.

To dye goldenrod yellow: Place wet alum-mordanted wool in the dyebath and simmer for 30 minutes. Cool, rinse and dry.

To dye brass gold: Place wet chrome-mordanted wool immediately in a cooled dyebath and simmer for 30 minutes. Cool, rinse, and dry.

Coreopsis

Locations found: Fields in eastern North America and California.

To prepare dye: Cover 8 ounces of torn flowers and stems with water.

To dye orange: Add wet alum-mordanted wool to the plant and water mixture. Simmer for about 15 minutes and let it cool overnight in the ooze. Rinse and dry.

To dye red-orange: Follow the above steps, but after the wool is removed from the ooze, dip it in an ammonia afterbath, rinse, and dry.

Nightshade

Locations found: Wasteplaces throughout the United States and Canada.

To prepare dye: Cut up 1 pound of nightshade plants and cover with water.

To dye rich yellow: Place wet alum-mordanted wool in the bath and simmer for 30 minutes. Cool, rinse, and dry.

To dye golden yellow: Follow the above directions using chrome-mordanted wool.

Pigweed

Locations found: Throughout the United States and Canada.

To prepare dye: Cut up about 1 pound of pigweed plants, cover them with water, boil for 1 hour, and cool.

To dye moss green: Place wet alum-mordanted wool in the plant and water mixture, adding enough water to cover the yarn, and simmer for 40 minutes. Cool the wool overnight in the ooze, rinse, and dry.

To dye brass gold: Follow the above directions using chrome-mordanted wool.

Dyes from Cultivated Flowers

Dahlia

To prepare dye: Tear apart 3 quarts of fresh or dried flowers and cover them with water.

To dye burnt orange: Add chrome-mordanted wool to the flower-water mixture and simmer for 30 minutes. Let the mixture stand overnight to cool. Remove the wool and dip it in an ammonia after-bath, rinse, and dry.

Fig. 10-10   Dahlia.

Purple Crocus

To prepare dye: Tear apart 1/2 pound of flowers and cover them with water.

To dye green-blue: Place wet alum-mordanted wool in with the flowers and water. Heat and keep the water just below simmering for 30 minutes. Allow the wool to cool in the ooze overnight, rinse, and dry. The color may be darkened with an ammonia afterbath.

To dye light green: Follow the above directions using chrome-mordanted wool.

Fig. 10-11   Crocus.

Yellow Daffodils

To prepare dye: Cover about 1 pound of torn flowers with water.

To dye rich yellow: Place wet alum-mordanted wool in the plant and water mixture and simmer for 30 minutes. Cool the wool in the plant ooze overnight, rinse, and dry. To strengthen the color, dip the wool in an ammonia afterbath before rinsing.

To dye deep gold-yellow: Follow the above directions using chrome-mordanted wool.

Fig. 10-12   Daffodils.

Dyes from Foods

Onion Skins

To prepare dye: Boil 1/2 pound of red or yellow onion skins for 30 minutes and let the mixture cool. Strain out the solid matter and add enough water to the dye liquid to cover the wool.

To dye red-brown: Place wet alum-mordanted wool in a dyebath made from red onion skins and simmer for 45 minutes. Let it cool, rinse, and dry. To obtain greenish tones, place the yarn in an ammonia rinse.

To dye orange-brown: Follow the above directions using copper-mordanted wool.

To dye yellow or gold: Follow the above formulas, using yellow onion skins to prepare the dyebath.

Purple Cabbage

To prepare dye: Soak the alum-mordanted wool with about 1 pound of purple cabbage leaves in water overnight. Remove the wool and stir in 1 teaspoon salt.

To dye blue-lavender: Place the wool in the plant, salt, and water mixture and simmer for 40 minutes. Cool the wool overnight in the dyebath, rinse, and dry.

Dry Kidney Beans

To prepare dye: Cover 1 pound of red kidney beans with water and simmer for 30 minutes. Let the bath cool and strain out the beans.

To dye red-brown: Place wet alum-mordanted wool in the dyebath and simmer for 40 minutes. Let the water cool, rinse, and dry.

Dye Plants Requiring No Mordants

Black Walnut Hulls

To prepare dye: Soak 1/2 peck (4 quarts) of firm walnut hulls in water overnight. In the morning, boil for about 2 hours and let it cool. Strain out the hulls and add enough water to make the dyebath.

To dye walnut brown: Place wet unmordanted

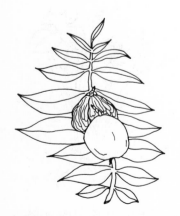

Fig. 10-13 Black walnut hulls.

wool in the dyebath and simmer 30 minutes. Let cool, rinse, and dry.

Sumac Berries

To prepare dye: Crunch 1/2 peck (4 quarts) of red sumac berries and soak in water overnight. In the morning, boil for 30 minutes, cool, and strain out the berries. Add enough water to cover the yarn and add 1/2 teaspoon copperas (iron sulfate) to the dyebath.

To dye grey: Place wet unmordanted wool in the bath and simmer for 30 minutes. Cool, rinse, and dry.

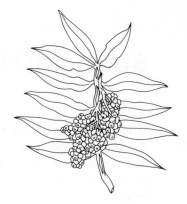

Fig. 10-14   Sumac berries.

Turmeric

To prepare dye: Dissolve 1 tin (2 ounces) of turmeric in hot water. Add 1 cup of vinegar and enough cool water to cover the wool.

To dye yellow-orange: Place wet wool in the turmeric, water, and vinegar mixture, and simmer for 30 minutes. Cool, rinse, and dry.

Some Fermentation Formulas

Brown Rock Lichen

To prepare ooze: Combine 1/4 cup broken-up lichens with a solution of 1/2 cup ammonia in 2 cups warm water. Place in a jar with a tight fitting lid and set aside for several weeks in a warm place (room temperature or slightly warmer is fine).

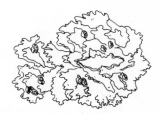

Fig. 10-15   Rock lichen.

To dye magenta-purple: Add a small amount of concentrated ooze to water to create the dyebath. Add the wet wool and simmer for 30 minutes. Cool overnight, rinse, and dry.

Pomegranate

To prepare ooze: Combine rinds and seeds of six pomegranates with water to cover in a jar with a loose fitting lid.

To dye orange-beige: Add wet wool to the mixture, cover loosely, and let stand in a warm place. Turn the yarn daily until the wool rinses clear in water. This will take about a week, depending upon the color desired.

Fig. 10-16   Pomegranate.

SUPPLIERS

Often a wealth of fiber supplies can be found in a local craft or yarn shop. Check the yellow pages of your telephone directory to locate those in your community, and investigate new shops as they arise. Sometimes a local spinner will sell through a craft shop; you may be surprised to find some exotic handspun fibers in your own town.

Yarns

Craft Yarns of Rhode Island
  P.O. Box 385
  Pawtucket, Rhode Island 02862

CUM
  5 Rosemersgrade
  1362 Copenhagen K
  Denmark

Dharma Trading Company
  P.O. Box 1288
  Berkeley, California 94701

Folklorico
  P.O. Box 625
  Palo Alto, California

Lily Mills Co.
  Handweaving Department
  Shelby, North Carolina 28150

The Mannings
  Creative Crafts
  East Berlin, Pennsylvania 17316

Tahki Imports
  336 West End Avenue
  New York, New York 10023

The Yarn Depot, Inc.
  545 Sutter Street
  San Francisco, California 94102

Yarn Primitives
  P.O. Box 1013
  Weston, Connecticut 06880

Weaving and Spinning Supplies

Leclerc Corporation
  P.O. Box 491
  Plattsburg, New York 12901

The Mannings
  Creative Crafts
  East Berlin, Pennsylvania 17316

School Products Company, Inc.
  1201 Broadway
  New York, New York 10001

The Craftool Company, Inc.
  1421 West 240th Street
  Harbor City, California 90710

Natural Dyes and Chemical Mordants

Dominion Herb Distributors, Inc.
  61 St. Catherine Street West
  Montreal 18, Canada

The Mannings
  Creative Crafts
  East Berlin, Pennsylvania 17316

Nature's Herb Company
  281 Ellis Street
  San Francisco, California 94102

Nature's Fibres
  109 Tinker Street
  Woodstock, New York 12498

SUGGESTED READING

Coutts, Lucele. *Baskets and Beyond.* New York: Watson-Guptill, 1977.

Creager, Clara. *Weaving.* New York: Doubleday, 1974.

Davenport, Elsie. *Your Handspinning.* Pacific Grove, California: Craft and Hobby Book Service, 1970.

Edson, Nicki Hitz, and Stimmel, Arlene. *Creative Crochet.* New York: Watson-Guptill, 1977.

Franck, Frederick. *The Zen of Seeing.* New York: Random House, 1973.

Grae, Ida. *Nature's Colors.* New York: Macmillan, 1974.

Harvey, Virginia. *Macrame: The Art of Creative Knotting.* New York: Van Nostrand Reinhold, 1967.

Kluger, Marilyn. *The Joy of Spinning.* New York: Simon and Schuster, 1971.

Lesch, Alma. *Vegetable Dyeing.* New York: Watson-Guptill, 1970.

Linsenmaier, Walter. *Insects of the World.* New York: McGraw-Hill, 1972.

Meilach, Dona Z. *Macrame: Creative Design in Knotting.* New York: Crown, 1971.

Richards, M. C. *Centering.* Middletown, Connecticut: Wesleyan University Press, 1962.

Saint-Exupery, Antoine de. *The Little Prince.* Tr. by Katherine Woods. New York: Harcourt Brace Jovanovich, 1943.

Schetky, Ethel Jane McD., ed. *Dye Plants and Dyeing.* Brooklyn, New York: Brooklyn Botanic Garden, 1964.

Seagroatt, Margaret. *Rug Weaving for Beginners.* New York: Watson-Guptill, 1972.

Sommer, Elyse, and Sommer, Mike. *A New Look at Crochet.* New York: Crown, 1975.

METRIC
CONVERSION TABLE

Ounces		Grams
$1/2$	·	14
1	·	28
2	·	57
3	·	85
4	·	113
5	·	142
10	·	284

Pounds		Kilograms
$1/2$	·	.2
1	·	.4
2	·	.9
3	·	1.4
4	·	1.8
5	·	2.3
10	·	4.5

Cups		Milliliters
$1/4$	·	59
$1/3$	·	79
$1/2$	·	118
$2/3$	·	158
$3/4$	·	177
1	·	237
2	·	475

Pints		Milliliters
$1/2$	·	237
1	·	475
2	·	950

Quarts		Liters
1	·	.95
2	·	1.90
3	·	2.85
4	·	3.80

Gallons		Liters
1	·	3.8
2	·	7.6
3	·	11.4
4	·	15.0

Teaspoons		Milliliters
$1/4$	·	1.25
$1/2$	·	2.50
$3/4$	·	3.75
1	·	5.00
2	·	10.00

Tablespoons		Milliliters
1	·	15
2	·	30
3	·	45
4	·	60
5	·	75

Inches		Centimeters
$1/2$	·	1.3
1	·	2.5
2	·	5.0
3	·	7.5
4	·	10.0
5	·	12.5
10	·	25.0

INDEX

Page numbers in **bold** refer to illustrations.

Draw-in, 88, 90, 96
Drop spindle
  dressing, 130–131
  types of, 129, 131
Dushanko-Dobek, Anne,
  fiberwork by, **118**
Dye formulas, 147–151
  colors
    blues, 149, 150
    browns, 150
    gray, 151
    greens, 148, 149
    oranges, 148, 149, 151
    purple, 151
    reds, 148, 150
    yellows, 148–150
  sources
    cabbage, 150
    coreopsis, 148
    crocus, 149
    daffodil, 149
    dahlia, 149
    goldenrod, 147–148
    kidney bean, 150
    lichen, 151
    nightshade, 148
    onion, 150
    pigweed, 148–149
    pomegranate, 151
    sumac, 151
    turmeric, 151
    walnut hull, 150–151
Dyeing, natural, 132–151
  equipment, 137–138
  fermentation method, 145,
    151
  mordanting, 139–142
  in ooze, 142–144
  in plant material, 143–145
  post-dyebath coloring,
    144–145
    blooming, 144–145
    rinses, 144
    saddening, 145
    top-dyeing, 144
  preparing dyebath, 142
  preparing dyestuffs, 142
  without mordants, 139,
    145, 150, 151
Dyer's recordbook, 145–147
Dyestuffs
  berries, 134, 151
  dried plants, 134, 135
  field flowers, 133, 147–149
  foods, 135–136, 150, 151

  garden flowers, 134, 149
  nonmordant, 139, 145,
    150, 151
  sources of, 132–137
  supply houses, 136–137,
    152
  trees, 134, 150

"Earth Strata," 92–97

"Factory Town," 81–83
Fermentation dyeing, 145,
  151
Fibers, natural, 6–9
  animal, 6
  durability of, 8
  elasticity of, 7–8
  plant, 6
  ply of, 7
  rigidity of, 8–9
Figure 8 stitch, 53–54
Filler cord, 16
Fleece, 127, 129
"Flower," 74–78
"Forest Shrine," **118**
Found objects, 9–12, 88,
  112–114, 116–117
  natural, 9–11, 112–114
  manmade, 11–12, 87–88,
    116–117

Gallery of fiberworks,
  117–125
"Gargoyle," **122**
Geneslaw, Ruth, works by,
  120, 124
Ghiordes knot, 91, **92**
Glavé, Patricia McKenna,
  works by, **119, 122,
  123**
Gowell, Ruth, 74, **118**

Half knot, 17, **18**
Handspinning, 127–131
  carding, 129
  drop spinning, 129–131
  obtaining fleece, 127
  rolags, 129
  teasing, 128
Holding cord, 17
"Horse Feathers," **123**